Uniquely Woman

A STUDY ON PROVERBS 31:10-31

CATHY MCBRIDE

WESTBOW® PRESS
A DIVISION OF THOMAS NELSON & ZONDERVAN

Scripture taken from the HOLY BIBLE, NEW INTERNATIONAL VERSION®. Copyright © 1973, 1978, 1984 Biblica. Used by permission of Zondervan. All rights reserved.

Scripture taken from the King James Version of the Holy Bible.

WestBow Press books may be ordered through booksellers or by contacting:ww

WestBow Press
A Division of Thomas Nelson & Zondervan
1663 Liberty Drive
Bloomington, IN 47403
www.westbowpress.com
1 (866) 928-1240

Because of the dynamic nature of the Internet, any web addresses or links contained in this book may have changed since publication and may no longer be valid. The views expressed in this work are solely those of the author and do not necessarily reflect the views of the publisher, and the publisher hereby disclaims any responsibility for them.

Any people depicted in stock imagery provided by Thinkstock are models, and such images are being used for illustrative purposes only.
Certain stock imagery © Thinkstock.

ISBN: 978-1-4908-9078-4 (sc)
ISBN: 978-1-4908-9079-1 (e)

Print information available on the last page.

WestBow Press rev. date: 01/22/2016

This study is dedicated to my loving husband, Mark, who Is so very patient with me as I am still learning how to become 'Uniquely Woman'.

Contents

Part One

Meeting His Needs Mentally

Introduction

Who can find a virtuous woman?
For her price is far above rubies.
Proverbs 31:10

Leah gathered the dried flax and sat down on the roof of Aunt Lydia's small house. Lydia was entertaining company and Leah knew she needed to give them some privacy. Many women came to buy Aunt Lydia's beautiful cloth and often stayed to have her teach them about the scriptures. Many of them seemed so hungry to hear Lydia explain the scriptures to them. Leah touched the gold band on her right index finger. She thought about Benjamin and the night they had become betrothed. She smiled as she remembered the way her heart had jumped when she heard the knock at her door. Who would she find on the other side? She had been surprised when Papa told her that she had been chosen as a wife for someone very special. "This young man will make you a fine husband," Papa had said. "His father has chosen you out of all the other young women in the village for his son." She had felt as if her legs would surely give way beneath her when she saw him standing before her. Benjamin! Could it really be Benjamin? He was the last young man she had expected to see because everyone thought Benjamin would marry Sarah. When she and Sarah had walked through the village together, they often passed Benjamin as he came in from his boat after a morning of fishing. Leah thought he was beautiful. He was tall, very well built, and the red in his beard framed the red in his sun-kissed cheeks. He would smile but his eyes were always on Sarah. Leah was convinced that Benjamin did not know she existed, but here she sat with the betrothal ring on her finger.

After becoming betrothed, Leah had been sent from her home to the nearby village where Aunt Lydia lived. Mama and Papa had wanted her to spend this betrothal time with Aunt Lydia because she was a widow and they felt it would be good for both of them. Leah could learn so much from Lydia about cooking and making beautiful threads and cloth. Surely Benjamin would be pleased to have a wife with these abilities. It would take Benjamin about a year to prepare their home and then he would come for her during the night where she would be ready and waiting. She had learned so much more from Lydia than she had expected. Lydia had read Proverbs 31 to her every day. Verse 10 from this passage rang in her ears now as she sat quietly on the roof.

*"**Who can find a virtuous woman?**
For her price is far above rubies."*

*"This verse is the end of the story," Lydia had said. Leah wasn't exactly sure what Aunt Lydia meant but she knew she wanted to 'be' this verse; to be a virtuous woman. She wanted to be priceless for Benjamin and Lydia had begun to teach her. "It will take time, Leah," she had said. "It will happen through the seasons of your life with Benjamin, but you have to trust God in everything." "Are you ready to **serve** Benjamin?" Lydia had asked me. I was ready. I loved Benjamin and he had chosen me. Surely that was enough, wasn't it?*

1

$\mathcal{P}$riceless $\mathcal{T}$reasure

Have you ever seen a movie that began at the end? You Know. You have seen those movies where the characters are older at the start, and then, the rest of the story takes you back to what happened while they were younger. Well, that is exactly what we have in Proverbs 31:10. This verse is actually the end of the story.

The virtuous woman is a priceless treasure. Her price is far above rubies. She has followed the design in the remaining verses of this passage. It did not happen overnight, but rather through the seasons of her life, as she trusted God and His plan for her. The rest of this study will take you back through her life to show you how she became so priceless. You will find the virtuous woman as you see the virtues in her life that make her uniquely woman.

The word virtuous is translated to mean 'a force'. A truly virtuous woman is a force that is comparable to an army of men. Wow! That is exciting and scary at the same time. Her resources are numerous and we will discover what they are as we proceed through the passage. The root word refers to 'standing proudly in the midst of battle'. You will discover why this translation is relevant as we continue the study.

The word price is translated as her 'value', which is considered to be greater than rubies. Rubies were one of twenty-two precious stones mentioned in the bible. They were precious and desirable because of rarity, hardness, and beauty. (1) (Holman Bible Dictionary) The virtuous woman is all of these things. All of her virtues and resources fall under one of these three categories. This is why she is considered to be priceless.

The theme of the book of Proverbs is 'The Fear of the Lord'.

Read and write the following verses:

Proverbs 9:10

Proverbs 8:11

From these two verses, we can determine that the first two resources we find in the virtuous woman are:

1. A _____ of the _____

2. W __ __ __ __ m

These two virtues are the foundation for her great value.

In my study of Proverbs 31:10, God has led me to the story of a remarkable woman named Ruth.

Stop now and read the book of Ruth:

Pray that God will open this familiar story in a new and exciting way for you. Watch carefully for the virtues in Ruth's life.

Ruth gives us a picture of faithfulness and commitment in a relationship. Ruth's virtuous qualities were very rare during that time. We know this because in Ruth 2:11, Boaz tells Ruth all about her life since her husband's death. He says, "It has been showed me..." In other words, Ruth is the talk of the town. Why? She does the unthinkable! She lives her life to serve another. Boaz even tells her in verse 3:11, "...for all the city of my people doth know thou art a virtuous woman." What we discover in Ruth is the third precious virtue which is:

3. A s __ __ f l __ __ s sp __ __ __ t

How do we know Ruth had this precious, selfless spirit? In the first chapter of Ruth, we learn that Naomi, Ruth's mother-in-law, has become widowed. We need to understand how Naomi felt at this time in her life and why. In Ruth 1:20, she says, "...call me not Naomi, call me Mara: for the Almighty has dealt very bitterly with me..." The word Mara is translated as 'bitter'.

Here we have an aging, bitter, depressed woman. She is feeling extremely sorry for herself and can only see that God has removed everything from her life that she considered good and to have come from Him. She obviously wants everyone to know that she has every intention of wallowing in her bitterness. Have you ever spent time with anyone like this? Complaining constantly, a bitter person is no delight to be around.

Name all the reasons why Naomi was bitter:

Naomi also expressed sarcasm to Ruth on top of the bitterness when she said, "...are there any more sons in my womb that they may be your husband?" Poor Ruth! This woman she wanted to stay with was no picnic.

We are not given Ruth's reasons for remaining with Naomi. I believe it is very possible that Ruth had seen a glimpse of God in Naomi and her family that gave her a desire for more. In Ruth 1:16, she worded her desire beautifully.

Write Ruth 1:16

I believe Ruth viewed her relationship with Naomi as the key to a relationship with God. Imagine that! Choosing God in a time when things looked the darkest and most uncertain, rather than bailing out to seek happiness elsewhere. What a concept! Yet, this is truly the basis for your life as a virtuous woman of God. When was the last time you felt like bailing out? Picture your circumstances. Were they any worse than those of a woman who had lost everything she loved and was left with a bitter, old woman? Yet, freedom was not as desirable to her as a God she had glimpsed in the family of this woman named Naomi. We see in chapters 2-4, Ruth's faithfulness and commitment to God and to Naomi and how it led them both to find God had not forsaken them, but had a beautiful plan for their lives.

The foundation of a virtuous woman is the fear of the Lord. This fear of the Lord is the basis for a selfless spirit, a spirit willing to serve another under any circumstance for no other reason than the love of God. We find no indication in this passage that Ruth had any selfish expectations or motives for her commitment to Naomi.

Let's see what Jesus tells us about this kind of selfless spirit.

Write Matthew 10:39:

Ruth could have gone back to the security of the family she had known before her marriage, yet she somehow sensed the life she needed and desired existed in a relationship with God and a woman named Naomi. Ruth found her life, the life that God intended for her when she gave it up to *serve* God and a woman named Naomi.

As we proceed through the remaining verses of this passage in Proverbs, we will often refer back to Ruth. I am convinced that God intended this passage in Proverbs as a picture for our lives as Godly women. It was written for the young single man as a guideline for finding and choosing a Godly wife. So, what we have here is exactly what the man needs from his wife. That is the reason we need to discover and follow this design. However, I also feel we must take it from the beginning to the end as puzzle pieces. I am certain that God never intended for this passage to be treated like a Sunday buffet where we pick and choose the verses we think will fit into our lifestyle. Together, from the beginning to the end, we will see a beautiful picture of a life God designed for us as women. Are you truly ready to see this picture? Before you proceed, I urge you to drop to your knees in prayer.

Pray this prayer based on Matthew 13:23:

Feel free to add anything you feel is needed for you.

Dear God, I pray for a willing heart. I pray that I will hear God's word, understand, and bear fruit according to what I have learned.

2

Trusting Hearts

The heart of her husband doth safely
Trust in her, so that he shall have no
Need of spoil. Proverbs 31:11

L*eah smiled as she awoke to see Benjamin lying next to her. She remembered the night before when she awoke to hear him calling her name. "Leah, my love! Leah, my wife! The time is here, Leah. I've come to take you home!" Her friend, Sarah, quickly lit her lamp and awoke the other bridesmaids. They followed Benjamin to the home he had prepared for Leah. Soon after entering their new home, the marriage was consummated and they went out to join the others for a wonderful celebration. She could not be happier, it just wasn't possible.*

Sunlight began to sneak through the windows and for the first time, Leah could see the home Benjamin had prepared for her. She saw a small table with the beautiful linens she and Lydia had made for her new home. She also saw the lovely pottery plates and cups she had admired when she and mama had been out shopping a few weeks ago. Her favorite dress and cloak were hanging on the wall next to the door. She was amazed at how many of her things were already here and she wondered how Benjamin had retrieved them without her knowledge. Then, in the far corner she saw the most beautiful spinning wheel she had ever seen. She could tell it wasn't brand new, but she didn't care. She couldn't wait to go out and begin finding and gathering flax to dry on their roof. Would she enjoy sitting on the edge of their roof as much as she had enjoyed Lydia's? Sitting on the roof was something she loved doing after spreading out the flax stalks to dry or when she went up to gather them after they had dried. She would show Benjamin all she had learned about soaking and separating the flax fibers, then spinning the fibers into beautiful threads.

Leah looked down at Benjamin and saw him smiling up at her. She smiled at him and began to realize that she wasn't sure who this man really was. What would their life be like and could she please him? Last

13

night he had called for her, "Leah, my love!" Would he always be able to love her? Surely she could 'serve' this beautiful man and be the best wife Benjamin could imagine.

"The home you have prepared for us is perfect. I want to be a good wife for you, Benjamin," she said as she stared down at his face. "You will be fine, Leah," he said with a smile. My father has told me all about you, and he said your time with Lydia has made you into a fine wife, not just because you can help provide for our family, but also because you love God. My father says your love for God is what will make you the best wife for me and will allow me to trust in you with all my heart."

Leah suddenly felt a lump in her throat and a wave of fear swirled around inside of her. Benjamin said he trusted her because of her love for God. What did that mean and how would she know how to always make him trust in her? Proverbs 31:11 flooded her thoughts:

**"The heart of her husband doth safely trust in her,
so that he shall have no need of spoil."**

She remembered Lydia telling her that God had created her for Benjamin and that she was to be his helpmeet as she daily served him. That was it! She would make sure he had everything he needed and then he would always trust in her, or was it that his trust in her was everything that he needed? This was all very confusing to Leah right now but her doubts quickly faded as Benjamin pulled her close to him.

Leah knew she would think about this later, but for now she would lose herself in this beautiful man God had brought into her life. She had trusted God to provide a husband and he had far exceeded her hopes and dreams with Benjamin. She was convinced they would always feel the way they did right now and that everything would be perfect.

Safely Trust in Her

Do you think your husband, in all honesty, could say, "I safely trust in her, my wife."? Do you realize the deep gravity of those words? The '*heart*' of her husband is translated in Hebrew as referring to the feelings, the will, and even the intellect. The '*heart*' literally refers to the center of everything that is important to a man's life. The word '*trust*' is translated as confident or sure and to take refuge. The word '*spoil*' refers to his lacking in nothing of value. He has every confidence in her ability to meet his needs mentally, emotionally, physically, and spiritually.

In order for your husband to trust in you and have no lack of gain, you must first come to understand your unique creation and purpose as a woman. It is here that we must go back to the beginning, to the creation of the woman. In Genesis 2:18-25 we are told of the circumstances surrounding creation. God said in Genesis 2:18, "It is not good for man to be alone. I will make him a helper suitable for him." In verse 19 we discover that God, before creating this helper, chose to create all of the animals and then had Adam name them. It was then that Adam discovered for himself that he was alone. Verse 20 in Genesis chapter 2 says, "And the man gave names to all the cattle and to the birds of the sky and to every beast of the field, but for Adam there was not found a helper suitable for him. " Why did God allow Adam to experience his need before filling his need? I believe God knew the man needed to realize the significance of the woman he would create for him. He needed to experience that void in his life that could only be filled by the woman whom God made suitable for him.

The New Testament reiterates the unique purpose for our creation. "For man is not of the woman, but the woman of the man. Neither was the man created for the woman, but the woman for the man." 1 Corinthians 11:8-9. Beverly LaHaye, in her book The <u>Desires of a Woman's Heart</u> (2) says, "Unless we can accept the bible's teaching that woman was created for man, we cannot begin to follow God's plan for happy marriages. Denial of this truth may be the first step of rebellion against God's plan for marriage."

So, why not make this the first step toward a happy, joy-filled marriage? Come to understand that you were created because God looked down and saw that the man he created needed a suitable helper. Thus, we were created for a very unique purpose. When was the last time you thanked God for creating you and giving you the opportunity to be a companion or helpmeet for your husband?

Stop and do this right now! Ask God to show you the following:

What people or things in your life are getting in the way of your opportunity to be there for your husband? Begin listing them here.

Remember, he is supposed to come first according to scripture. God ordained that Adam and Eve "Be fruitful and multiply..." in Genesis 1:28. Children were and are to be part of the woman's life, but remember, you were first created to be a wife. How often do you allow your children's needs to take precedence over your husband's needs?

Many women feel called to have careers, but is that career draining you and keeping you from being there for your husband? Genesis 1:28 also says, "And God said to ***them***, be fruitful and multiply, and replenish the earth, and subdue it: and have dominion over the fish of the sea, and over the fowl of the air, and over every living thing that moveth upon the earth." Did you notice that God said, "… to them…"? The woman was commanded to be right alongside her man in his daily dominion over the earth. She was to have an active part in his life and his work as a helpmeet for him. When was the last time you took an active part in your husband's work or realized that everything you do for him, whether big or small, plays an active part in all that he does?

If you haven't been an active part of your husband's life, what do you think you could do to change this?

Some of my most exciting career opportunities came when I was willing to give up a career rather than allow it to hinder my calling as a suitable helper for my husband. God has allowed many opportunities throughout the years for me to work at home, part time, and even fulltime without having to bump my husband down to second place. Remember Matthew 10:39? I encourage you to write it in the margin!

Let's take all of this and correlate it to our virtuous woman, Ruth. In Ruth 2:12, Ruth's future husband, Boaz, says, "The Lord recompense thy work and a full reward be given thee of the Lord God of Israel under whose wings thou art come to trust." A husband's trust in his wife is neatly packaged in this verse. Boaz has become attracted to Ruth because he recognizes her trust in and dependence on God. He sees inner beauty in her. Ruth depended on God even when she had every reason to turn from Him. No woman can be who or what she needs to be for her husband without first having a strong desire for God in her life. A husband can only trust in his wife when she completely trusts in God. Trusting in God is trusting and believing His word whether you like it or not. Trusting God's word is to accept His purpose for your creation.

Boaz said Ruth had come under God's wing and he referred to Him as the God of Israel. The Psalmist in Psalm 91 writes, "He shall cover thee with His feathers and under His wings shalt thou trust: His truth shall be thy shield and buckler." God's truth is found only in His word where we are to daily 'take refuge'! We can't trust in God without trusting His precious word and seeking God in His word. When was the last time you *'began'* your day by seeking God in his word? The virtuous woman accepts God's word as truth, seeks Him daily, trusts in Him, and is painfully aware of her need for Him.

Proverbs 31:11 says that "her husband's heart safely trusts in her so that he will have no lack of gain."

Write Genesis 2:20:

God created you to be a suitable helper. His word, which you are to trust in, will give you everything you need to make this possible. If you are daily seeking God in prayer and bible study, then God will meet with you, grow you, and allow you to become all that you need to be so that you are able to fulfill your purpose. Your relationship with God is directly related to your ability to meet your husband's needs. You see, it is something you cannot do on your own, but only as you take refuge under the protective wings of the God you trust. As you do this, your husband can confidently begin to find refuge as you meet his needs.

Boaz found that kind of trust in Ruth. Ruth had chosen to put God first in her life and trust Him for everything. I tell you today that no man can live unhappily or without seeing a picture of Christ, when he lives with a woman who puts God first in her life. I believe he will learn to trust in her and in her God. Let's write *Matthew 10:39* this way:

> "And (she) that loseth (her) life
> (By accepting My purpose for her creation)
> For My sake will find it."

3

Open Doors

"She will do him good and not evil all the days of her life." Proverbs 31:12

Leah sat in the corner, looking out the open window as she was spinning. She thought of verses 1 and 2 in Psalms 89 and she began to sing,

"I will sing of thy steadfast love, O Lord, forever; with my mouth I will proclaim thy faithfulness to all generations. For thy steadfast love was established forever, thy faithfulness is firm as the heavens."

Leah loved making up tunes for the Psalms, especially when she was spinning. Leah also loved spinning and the women in her village had learned of the beautiful threads she made. They often came to buy them from her. She loved sitting at her spinning wheel in the mornings while Benjamin was out fishing.

Leah's family and Benjamin's family were converted Jews. They became believers when the apostle Paul had come through their village a few years earlier. Leah suddenly remembered that Mama wanted them to come for a prayer gathering and fellowship at their home that night and to meet some new believers. When Benjamin came in, she shared excitedly about the gathering and her desire for them to go. "You go without me Leah. I am traveling to the next village tonight so that I can fish on the other side of the lake tomorrow morning," said Benjamin.

"But Benjamin, you have not been to a prayer gathering in weeks," Leah said. "Why will you not go with me?"

"My job is to provide for our family and the child we have on the way," he said calmly.

"Benjamin, please tell me why must you always work so much and so hard?" Leah asked. Benjamin turned to her and she found herself bothered by the look in his eyes. She had not seen this look in him before. What did it

mean? She watched him as he packed some bread, then he looked at her and said, "I will be home late tomorrow night." He turned and left without saying goodbye, something else he had never done before. The joy she had felt only moments before had melted into despair as she thought about Benjamin and the look on his face. She watched and waited, so sure he would walk back in, grab her in his arms, and tell her he was sorry for putting work before her and God, but the room remained silent.

Leah tried to return to her spinning but she couldn't stop the tears. What had she done to upset Benjamin? Her thoughts turned to Proverbs 31 and she found herself reciting it aloud, "She will do him good and not evil all the days of her life". She stopped as she thought about the words in verse 12. The word 'evil' stung at her heart as she said it over again. That word, evil, explained exactly how she felt as she looked into Benjamin's eyes. Had she done him 'evil'? She had only meant to do him good by reminding him of his need for God and time with his family. Wasn't that part of her 'job' as helpmeet? As the tears continued to fall, Leah remembered something the apostle Paul had said. He had told them that God had set forth a very strong chain that would become very weak if ever it was altered. The chain began with God, connected to Christ, then the man, and finally to the woman or wife. Paul had talked about the importance of a woman's place in her husband's life. He had compared her to a door that could help him find his way to God. Leah had been confused and didn't understand how a woman could be a door 'between' her husband and God if she was 'under' him in this 'chain' of command.

Suddenly it began to make sense. As long as she remained 'under' her husband, he could clearly see and hear God's voice and the door remained 'open'. When she had tried to be the voice of God for her husband, she had moved between Benjamin and God, thus closing or blocking that way. She had 'altered' the chain and made it weak!

She had been crying and feeling sorry for herself all day and night. Now, she couldn't wait for Benjamin to come home. She wanted desperately to tell him she was sorry and that she had been so wrong.

Open the Door

The word 'do' in Proverbs 31:12 are translated to benefit or requite. To requite refers to repayment or retaliation for a wrong that has been done. It also refers to serving, yielding, and toiling. To 'do him good' refers to the woman's ability to serve, yield and toil in order to bring every good thing into her husband's life.

The word evil is translated as adversity, calamity, affliction, distress, harm, misery, and trouble. This translation for evil is taken from a root word which means to make 'good for nothing'.

We have seen how God's creation for us has given us a unique and precious Kingdom purpose as a helpmeet. However, God's creation required specific order. God has a unique calling for you as a woman. This calling begins when we accept not only our purpose in creation, but also our place in the God-given chain of command. I have heard my pastor, P. J. Scott, say that anything with two heads is a monster. Are you weary today because you are trying to live in a monstrous marriage? God has placed you under the authority of the man for a reason. The marriage relationship is in need of a spiritual leader. God chose the man for this position. However, your position is no less in God's eyes. Elisabeth Elliot (3) says, "This is not a position of aptitude, but rather a position of appointment." 1 Corinthians 11:3 says,

> "But I would have you know that the head of
> Every man is Christ; and the head of
> Every woman is the man;
> And the head of Christ is God."

Draw a triangle below. Inside the triangle, 'order' the following according to God's chain of command: woman, man, God, Christ

Does this verse affect our relationship with Christ? Not at all! Read Galatians 3:28.

> "There is neither Jew nor Greek...
> There is neither male nor female;
> For ye are ***all one*** in Christ Jesus."

This verse does not refer to your relationship with man, but to your relationship with God. It does not give you a basis for coming out from under the authority of your husband, but rather a basis for a wonderful relationship with God.

We are all one in Christ Jesus. Your direct line to Christ is no different from your husband's. God loves you, needs you, hears you, and answers your prayers only on the basis of who you are in *Him*. Your gender does not affect your relationship with Him. How beautiful and comforting to know that God sees me and desires a relationship with me as an heir to His Kingdom, not because of what I am, but rather whose I am.

Genesis 1:27 says, "So God created man in his own image, in the image of God created him; male and female created them." Relish in the knowledge that you were created in God's image as a woman.

Now is the time for you to stop and prayerfully consider your family situation. Have you usurped or come out from under your husband's authority and tried to take on the spiritual leadership of your home? If your answer is yes, write your reasons below.

I found myself answering yes to this question a number of years ago. My expectations for my husband led me to believe that he was not spiritually qualified. I placed myself above him, and ***unrightfully*** tried to take this position from him. Then I wondered why he began to grow away from the Lord.

We allow ourselves to become burdened over the fear of becoming a doormat in our marriage relationship or convince ourselves that we are more spiritually qualified. This, I believe, is the basis for our rebellion toward God's chain of command. We are afraid we will lose ourselves. But wait! Remember Matthew 10:39? Do you have it memorized yet? Write it in the margin once again.

Actually, when we are willing to lose ourselves, we become comparable to a door rather than a doormat. We are a door that stands between our husbands and God. When I tried to usurp authority over my husband, I began closing that door. Not only was I attempting to rearrange ***God's*** chain of command to suit ***my*** expectations, I was also moving away from my ability to be a helpmeet.

In Genesis 2:15-17, we find the account of God's command to Adam that he not eat of the tree of knowledge of good and evil. We find Eve repeating this command to the serpent in Genesis 3:3-4. You will notice that she tells the serpent that, God said...." She was very aware of the origin of the command. Eve was deceived, however, into believing that the serpent's direction for her life was more profitable than the direction she had received from her God. Therefore, Eve usurped God's authority over her and also her husband's authority by taking the forbidden fruit. Not only that, but she moved away from her ability to be a suitable helpmeet by leading her husband into sin, thus closing the door between Adam and God. No longer would Adam enjoy the relationship for which he had been created. Eve's disobedience resulted in the chain of command when God told her in Genesis 3:16, "...and he shall rule over thee."

Here we find the reason for the translation of 'do' in Proverbs 31:12. We are destined to requite or repay our husbands for the sin of the woman in the Garden of Eden. Our responsibility as women is great. We have amazing influence on our husbands. God can use us to bring our husbands back into fellowship with Himself when we open our doors.

Have you ever wondered how Eve could have so easily given up all she had for a bite of fruit? Have you found yourself being judgmental of her ability to believe the serpent's lies with so little restraint? Every day we make decisions that choose our own selfish desires over that which we know God would have us do. It is called disobedience. When we alter the chain of command we are disobeying God. God commanded our obedience to our husbands when He placed us under them in His chain of command. When we choose to live in disobedience, we are doing our husbands evil and not good.

The tree of knowledge of good and evil was Eve's downfall. She did her husband evil and not good when she came out from under him and made the 'spiritual' decision for him. Unless you accept God's chain of command and live by its direction, you will not be able to do your husband 'good' all the days of your life.

If you are thinking that you can't do this, you are absolutely right. Neither can I.

Write Philippians 4:13 below:

You will need to daily take yourself and empty your selfish desires before the Lord. Only then can God fill you with Himself so that you can pour Him out on your husband.

Let's write Matthew 10:39 this way:

> "...And (she) that loseth (her) life
> (by accepting her place in God's chain
> of command) for my sake will find it."

4

Closed Hands

She seeketh wool and flax and
worketh willingly with her hands.
Proverbs 31:13

Leah held little Abigail on her hip as she moved around their home and attended to the daily chores. Leah sang the first two verses from Psalms 128:

"Blessed is everyone who fears the Lord, who walks in His ways!

You shall eat of the fruit of the labor of your hands;

You shall be happy, and it shall be well with you."

Abigail was singing too. She clapped her hands as she sang and watched her Mama's face for approval. Benjamin walked in and began singing with them as he reached for the arms extending toward him from Abigail's small frame. "This is one of the first songs your mama taught me," he said to Abigail.

"I thought it was time this morning," said Leah as she rubbed the large protruding bump under her dress. Benjamin's eyes grew excited and then concerned as he watched Leah continuing her work. Shouldn't you be resting, Leah?" he asked. "You know you don't need to carry Abigail around. She is quite able to walk now," he gently reminded her. Leah sat down as she realized how concerned Benjamin was about her condition. "I have arranged for Lydia to be here by the end of the week. She can help you with Abigail and the house until the baby comes," said Benjamin. "But, Benjamin, I am fine!" said Leah. "I will go crazy if I have to sit all day and unable to take care of our home, and how can I make my beautiful thread if I can't go out to seek the flax I need?" Benjamin knelt beside her and said, "Lydia will help with what is needed. Please slow down until she arrives."

Leah tried very hard to hide her disappointment, but Benjamin realized there was something wrong. "What," he asked as he looked directly into her eyes. "I almost had enough money to buy the basket I wanted for the new baby's crib," said Leah. The new baby will have no place to sleep and Abigail's bed is much too small for the two of them." Benjamin looked down at the floor. "You didn't tell me you were saving for a crib basket, Leah," he said. "You know I haven't been catching as many fish lately and we need to save our money for other things right now. I really need for you to put the basket out of your thoughts for now. We will work something out for the baby. Everything will be fine."

Leah watched as Benjamin took Abigail outside to play. She thought about all of her hard work. She enjoyed working for her family, but couldn't she have something she wanted just this once? As she became aware of her unhappiness, she realized that the only time she ever felt this way was when she was unable to have her own way about something. Leah closed her eyes and prayed, "Lord, you know my desire to have a basket crib for the new baby so the baby and Abigail can both sleep without distraction. Lord, the basket is big enough for the baby to sit and play as it grows, I would be able to continue my spinning and other chores around the house, and easily carry the basket when I go out to seek flax. Lord, you have taught me that all things are possible with you and I pray you will change my heart as I willingly release the money I was saving over to Benjamin."

Worketh Willingly

Our word study will be especially relevant with this verse. The word 'seeketh' is translated to show that she searched diligently and continually to find these two items. It was a repeated action.

The wool she sought was the fleece from animals, usually sheep. The fibers were used to make thread. The flax was a plant. The fibers from this plant were used to make thread for linen. The woman's process of making thread was very time consuming. However, the process of preparing the flax was quite a job in itself. The flax had to be found and picked. Then, it was dried on rooftops. After deseeding and soaking, it was redried. Then, a utensil much like a comb was used to separate the fibers. This combing and cleansing was done several times.

What we see here in Proverbs 31:13 is not so much this woman's use of wool and flax, but rather her willingness to work continually for her family. We don't grasp wool and flax today, but our hands grasp the mop, the vacuum cleaner, the broom, the dirty clothes, our children, etc., etc. When I began studying this verse, I must admit I was confused as I felt God was pointing to and picturing a woman's submission. I discovered the use of hands in Proverbs 31 is translated two different ways. The Hebrew translation used in verse 13 refers to the palm, hollow, or middle of the hand, much like a bowl or spoon. It actually represents a cupped or closed hand. The exact same translation is used in Exodus to describe the spoons or bowls used in the Holy of Holies inside the tabernacle. These bowls and spoons held the drink offerings used in the tabernacle. These drink offerings were taken from the blood of the acceptable sacrifices presented in the tabernacle. Slowly, but surely, I began to picture this woman with her cupped hands, grasping the wool and flax. Her work, the work of her 'closed', cupped hands, is an offering of herself.

Let's go back to Genesis, chapter three. After God told Eve that she would be under her husband's authority, Adam was told in Genesis 3:17, "...cursed is the ground for thy sake, in sorrow shalt thou eat of it all the days of thy life." The Hebrew translation for sorrow is to toil or labor. Adam would have to work for everything they would need.

The Hebrew translation for 'worketh' in Proverbs 31:13 also means to labor. Are you beginning to see, as I did, that the chain of command set forth in the garden pictured submission? The man was to be submissive to God as he labored to provide for his family. In the same way, the woman was to labor for her family in submission to her husband.

Write Ephesians 5:22-24:

In these verses we see how a wife's submission pictures the church to Christ. The chain of command actually puts you in a place of subjection. Through obedience we submit our will over to God as we live in submission to our husbands.

Are you beginning to get a glimpse of this beautiful picture? If you are still having trouble with this picture, let me remind you that we have only just begun to put the pieces together, so please stay with me.

Submission to your husband is in direct relation to your obedience to God. Submit to your husband, and you obey God. Obey God and your life comes into focus.

Do you remember from 1 Corinthians 11:3, we see that Christ himself was in the chain of command as we read, "...and the head of Christ is God." We see Christ's submission and obedience pictured beautifully in Luke 23:46 when he says, "...Father, into thy hands I commend my spirit." This was Jesus' last earthly act of obedience to his heavenly Father. My pastor preached a stirring message on this passage while I was working on this chapter and I was able to see how it all tied together. The Greek translation for hands in this verse is the same as the Hebrew translation in Proverbs 31:13. It refers to the same hollowness for grasping. Can't you somehow picture God tightly grasping, with those closed hands, the spirit of his precious son as he, "...gave up the ghost", Luke 23:46? The sacrificial offering of submission that God held in his hands that day was His son. This precious sacrifice was made for you and for me. Jesus Christ is the woman's perfect example of submission in its purest form.

Write Matthew 10:39:

Perfect submission is not possible without death. For the woman, this death is the daily act of yielding herself in service to meet her husband's needs and care for her family.

Consider Matthew 10:39 the key as you begin opening the door of submission in your marriage. Pray daily that God will continue to bring this verse into focus for you, therefore clearing the picture **He** has for your marriage. God can and will show you how to lose your life on a daily basis.

In her book, <u>The Desires of a Woman's Heart</u>, (4) Beverly LaHaye says of a woman, "Her position of submission is surprisingly powerful. As women after God's own heart we are to use our position of submission in our husband's lives to build, strengthen, encourage, and support them."

This power of submission is possible with 'closed' hands. The translation for hands in Proverbs 31:13 also refers to power. But, this power comes only through the relinquishing of your own power. When you are able to relinquish the power you might be holding over your husband, you are given a much greater power by God.

As Jesus hung on the cross that day, those who knew Him wondered why he didn't call on the power they had so often seen Him use to heal and even resurrect the dead. But, that day, in His submission to his heavenly Father, He relinquished His power, providing an even greater power. Jesus Christ's power of submission, through death, provided us with eternal life as he took our sin on the cross with Him that day at Calvary.

Proverbs 31:13 also says, "...she worked *willingly* with her (submissive) hands." She was eager and often found pleasure in serving her husband and family. It's true we don't work with wool and flax to make our own fabric today, but every day we are in position to offer ourselves in service to our husband and family.

We have seen already that our virtuous woman, Ruth, had a submissive spirit.

Write Ruth 1:17:

What is Ruth willing to do *with* Naomi in this verse?

Ruth is again expressing her desire for God and a servant's spirit to Naomi and her God as opposed to going her own way. ***Submission is the opposite of going your own way.*** Ruth even expresses her desire for God to deal severely with her if she is unable to keep this commitment. Ruth is willing to die to herself in service to Naomi.

Let's write Matthew 10:39 this way.

> "...and she that loseth her life,
> (Through submission to her husband)
> For my sake, shall find it."

Which way are you going today? You will discover as you begin moving from 'going your own way' that you will actually begin to *find* your way as Jesus tells us in this verse. I can tell you from experience that it is an exciting and amazing journey, unlike the confusion I experienced from going my own way.

5

Keen Senses

She is like the Merchant ships; she bringeth
Her food from afar. Proverbs 31:14

L eah watched Levi as he kicked his little legs and smiled at her. God had blessed her with two precious children. She was sad as she remembered that this would be Lydia's last day with them before she returned home. Leah had actually enjoyed being pampered by Lydia and would miss her company. There was a knock at the door and her friends Sarah and Rebekah appeared. "My father is taking us across the lake to shop in one of the lake front villages. Leah, come and go with us while Lydia is still here to watch the babies," said Sarah. "We must go now if we are to be home by dark." Leah was unsure as she glanced at Lydia. "Go with your friends," smiled Lydia. "This will be good for you." Leah grabbed her cloak and kissed everyone goodbye as she quickly ran out the door. It was very exciting to go to a village where she had never been before. Leah had heard about the exotic foods and merchandise in these villages because they were closer to the sea where the ships came in and out, and very little of this merchandise ever made it to their village. Leah was amazed not only at the amount of merchandise, but the prices were so much more affordable than they were at home. "They have so much merchandise arriving here in bulk that they must sell quickly," said Sarah's father. "The sellers must be rid of it before more comes in on the ships." Sarah squealed as she saw a crib basket that was much bigger than the one she had been saving for and it was less than half the price. Maybe she would buy it before they left for the day. As she walked through the streets she was amazed at the exotic fruits and vegetables that she had never seen before and the sellers were very anxious to supply samples. They were all so delicious. Leah remembered how much Benjamin loved fruit and he wished they could afford more of it for their family. There was dried beef in bulk for almost nothing, enough to last months. Leah could not believe how quickly the day went by and she held her purchases tightly as they made their way back home across the lake.

Lydia smiled at Leah as she helped her unpack her purchases. "You were a very wise shopper today,' said Lydia. "Benjamin will be so proud of you."

"I hope so," said Leah, "I have heard him say so often what he enjoys eating and I hope he likes the new net I found for him. He has lost so many fish lately because of the holes in his old net. Sarah's father said the price was amazing. "

Benjamin came home and saw the meal of fruit, vegetables, and dried beef and was pleasantly surprised. They had not had fruit in weeks. Benjamin smiled as he listened to Leah tell about her day and how little she had spent for her purchases. Tears came to his eyes as he opened a package and saw the new net. "This net will bring us more money," he said as he held Leah tightly.

Leah awoke the next morning and found Lydia packing her things to leave. "Benjamin left very early this morning," she told Leah. "He said he would like to get home earlier today since I am leaving to go home. I will miss you all very much. Leah, I am so proud of you for serving Benjamin and making him a priority in your life. He told me this morning how much it means to him that he can trust in you as a wife and mother. Leah, you are learning what it means to lose yourself in order to serve another and that is what submission is all about." Leah hugged Lydia tightly and tears came to her eyes as she watched her walk away. Having Lydia around made it so much easier to follow God's plan as a wife and mother, but she somehow felt as if she had made a major breakthrough. Leah smiled as she looked back at Levi while he lay quietly at the end of Abigail's small bed. Abigail had not complained once about sharing the bed with her new brother. Leah felt so full inside.

She bringeth her food from afar

When the Lord had brought me this far in my own quest for truth, I was faced with several major questions. How can I possibly know how to be a submissive helpmeet? Where do I begin as I strive to meet my husband's needs?

The word helpmeet in Genesis 2:18 showed the woman to be precisely adapted to man. When something is precise, it is distinguished from all others. It is neither more nor less than it should be, but rather perfect and complete.

The Hebrew translation for *meet* is suitable, comparable, or corresponding. While being made unique, you were also made to be like man in ways that make you comparable to him, and to become truly one with him. God made you precisely as you need to be in order to fulfill your purpose. This includes a built in ability to know how to go about it.

Dr. Adrian Rogers (5) says that as women, God has given us a very sophisticated radar system that allows us to be able to talk with someone and still know what is going on in all other directions around us. I believe he is absolutely right about this and that women have been gifted with very keen senses. Can you imagine the possibilities when we take this built in system and direct it as God leads?

We have already seen that God made you perfectly so that you are able to meet your husband's needs mentally, emotionally, physically, and spiritually. We know this is true because of what we discovered in Proverbs 31:11. Proverbs 31:14 refers to the woman who has learned to direct her keen senses and radar in order to be enterprising as she provides for her family.

The merchant ships of that time traveled far away in all directions seeking merchandise suitable for trading. They went the extra mile when necessary and often went into unfamiliar territory. This verse says the virtuous woman will go to the same extremes to find the best for her family. She is using those God-given senses and directing her radar as she travels the extra miles, or goes into unfamiliar territory to find the best for her family. Let's face it; can't you spot a bargain from a mile away? It is in our blood! God made us that way.

I have a friend who taught me to pray before shopping. When she began to do this, she never again paid full price for anything. She always found the items her family needed in ways that saved money. God was directing her radar, and she often found herself in places where she had never shopped, but would find something she was looking for. This practice has become a tremendous blessing to me. God has taught me that when he doesn't direct me to a bargain, I can usually be sure that the item is not something I need right away.

God has given you the same ability to discover your husband's needs. You must put all those keen senses to work and God will show you how to direct them. One of my favorite verses is Jeremiah 33:3. **Write it here:**

Don't you just love that? Have you ever wished you could just get inside your husband's mind to discover what he needs? Remember, God created you perfectly to meet your husband's needs. When you are uncertain, just ask your heavenly maker, and He will direct your radar accordingly.

I have discovered that one of my most helpful senses is hearing. When I take the time to listen to my husband, I hear much of what I need in order to know how to help him. I have discovered that when my husband, Mark, asks me to do something for him, he expects that I will take care of him by following through with his request. When he comes in at the end of the day, he will often ask right away if I took care of his request. When I am able to say yes, then he does not have to question that he is a priority in my life. If I say no, it will usually be followed by all of my excuses. He will not hear my excuses but rather that I cared more about meeting my own needs. He will not feel cared for.

Start a list of things you learn as you begin to listen to your husband.

What other senses do you believe you could use to make new discoveries about your husband's needs? How could you use them?

If you truly desire to meet your husband's needs out of obedience to God, he will surely direct your keen senses as you submissively begin to travel the extra miles into your husband's unfamiliar territory and discover what he needs. You may also be surprised at the joy you experience as you begin meeting your husband's needs and rightfully making him the priority he is supposed to be in your life. I hope you stop right now, drop to your knees, and pray for guidance as you begin your travels. God is waiting for you with the answers, but you must be ready to travel the extra miles and perhaps go where you have never gone before.

Let's write Matthew 10:39 this way.

> "…And (she) that loses (her) life
> (By traveling into unfamiliar territory)
> For my sake shall find it."

Write a prayer for your husband based on Jeremiah 33:3.

Are you prepared to pray this prayer every day?

Wrapping It Up:

Meeting His Needs Mentally

Discover Where He Is:

As we begin the process of becoming the helpmeet that God intended for us to be, we must go where our husband's needs begin.

If you remember, in chapter 2, we learned that our husband's 'heart' actually refers to the intellect, the will, and even the feelings. We saw how his heart is the basis or center of everything for the man. I believe a more accurate translation for Proverbs 31:11 could actually be "...his head trusts in her..." After all, this is where the intellect, the will and the feelings all begin. Any current, Christian psychologist will tell you that men are logical and analytical. Everything for the man centers on his mental process. For this reason, we must go here first if we are to successfully follow our calling of helpmeet.

There is a word in scripture that gives us the basis for our husband's 'mental' needs and his mental process revolves around this word. Ephesians 5:33 says "...and the wife must *respect* her husband."[NIV] *Respect* is the foundation for meeting your husband's needs mentally.

The Greek word for respect is phobeo. It is translated to be alarmed, to be in awe of, reverence, and is taken from a root word which means to be put in fear of. This means we are to think more highly of our husbands than is our *human* tendency.

The Greek word for 'must' is translated 'see' in the KJV as eido and it means mechanical, passive, or casual vision. Showing respect for your husband should be something you do as casually or naturally as brushing your teeth.

We have seen that a unique woman's life must begin with a fear of the Lord. Unlike Eve, she recognizes the consequences of disobedience, and is not easily deceived. In the same way, she is to respect or reverence her husband, by accepting her purpose of helpmeet and acknowledging him as her authority. She recognizes this as being directly related to her fear of the Lord. She is not to go through life fearing her husband, but rather the consequences of a life lived in service to herself rather than in service to her husband.

Respect for your husband begins by accepting your God given purpose of helpmeet and your position in the chain of command.

Meet Him Where He Is:

We are going to look carefully at the life of a Godly woman in scripture as we discover how to meet our husbands with respect.

> "Instead, it should be the unfading beauty of a
> Gentle and quiet spirit, which is of great worth
> In God's sight. For this is the way the holy
> Women of the past who put their hope in God
> Used to make themselves beautiful. They were
> Submissive to their own husbands, like Sarah
> Who obeyed Abraham and called him her master. You
> Are her daughters if you do what is right and do not
> Give way to fear. 1Peter 3:4-6

I believe that Sarah is one of our best examples in scripture of an obedient wife. Peter refers to her in Peter 3:4 as possessing a gentle and quiet spirit. The word gentle is from the Greek word praus, and is translated as meek, mild, and humble. The word quiet is from the Greek word hesuchios, and is translated as keeping one's seat, peaceable, and not prone to arguments. It is taken from a root word which means immovable as in steadfast or settled. She knows her place and has settled into it with comfort. Sarah was meek and peaceable, but you will see later that she could never be compared to a mouse. Sarah learned the hard way how to become obedient and respect her husband.

In verse six, Peter reminds us of Sarah's reference to Abraham as master. The Greek word is Kurios. It means supreme, in authority, controller, as a respectful title. She showed respect as she recognized her place in the chain of command. The Greek word for 'called' is Kaleo . It refers to calling aloud. It is taken from a root word meaning to 'hail' or 'urge on'. She shows respect to her husband by urging him on and she does this aloud so that he can *hear* her respect.

Verse six also refers to her obedience to her husband in everything. The word obey is from the Greek work hupakouo, and is translated to mean compliance or submission, attentive, and hearkening. It is taken from a root word meaning to listen attentively, to hear under as a subordinate, to heed or conform to a command. Again, she recognized him as her authority. She followed his leadership. Why? Because, in verse five, we see that Sarah and other holy women of the past "...put their hope in God." Sarah had learned the hard way throughout her long life that obedience to God, through respect for her husband, is the only way to have hope for the life we need as women.

Rest In Where You Are:

The word hope in verse five is translated as trusted in the KJV. It is from the Greek word elpizo[el-pid-zo] and means to expect, confide, have hope and trust. It is taken from a root word which means to anticipate, usually with pleasure; expectation or confidence, and faith. Sarah had learned to rest in her God with faith, hope and confidence.

Verse six also tells us that Sarah did not give way to fear. The word fear is the same Greek translation we saw for respect in Ephesians 5:33. Sarah was not ruled by her fear or her respect, but rather by her love and trust in God.

Sarah's confidence in God was evident because she had experienced his protection in her life. Genesis 12:17-20 gives us the account of God's protection for Sarah as we see her delivered from the house of Pharaoh where Abraham had sent her. If you remember, Abraham had asked Sarah to lie for him by saying she was his sister. She did not try to choose between her husband and God, but she obeyed her husband, thus obeying God, and found God waiting for her with his protection.

Sarah had also experienced the consequences of disobedience. In Genesis 16:1-6 we find the account of Sarah's impatience with God. She was unwilling to wait on the Lord for provision, so she gave her maid, Hagar, to Abraham, hoping that Hagar would provide the child she could not give her husband. Her disobedience and impatience affected Abraham, Sarah, Hagar, and Hagar's son Ishmael. The affects and the pain of this disobedience were long lasting.

In her old age, Sarah discovered the hope that comes in waiting on God's timing as she lived in submission and obedience to her husband.

Sarah had tried it her way, and God's way. She learned to respect her husband as she discovered the blessings and the hope that come when we choose God's way.

Part Two

Meeting His Needs Emotionally

6

Difficult Seasons

She riseth also while it is yet night;
And giveth meat to her household and a
Portion to her maidens. Proverbs 31:15

Leah lit her lamp and rose quickly as she awoke to the soft sobs announcing Levi's need for her. She held Levi close as he nursed, and she smiled with delight at the beautiful eyes that studied her with gratitude and contentment. Her delight quickly faded as she looked around her home and thought of the many things there were for her to do this day. She looked at the corner where her spinning wheel stood. She had done very little spinning since Levi arrived. Benjamin had been working more to make up for the money she could not provide with her threads. There was a very nice pile of flax fibers, Lydia had made sure of that before she left. Leah looked down at Levi to see his eyes closing as he fell back to sleep. She put him back down at the foot of the small bed he shared with his sister, Abigail. Leah's bed seemed to pull at her as she longed to climb in and sleep until the sunlight crept through the windows. Instead, she made her way to the corner where her spinning wheel stood. As she pulled the cover back from the window, the full moon flooded the corner with light. She sat down and began to spin. Leah couldn't sing aloud, but she found herself quietly reciting verses from Psalms 119:

"At midnight I rise to praise thee…The earth,
O Lord, is full of thy steadfast love; teach me thy statues."
Leah continued to recite verses from the same Psalms as she prayed for her family:
For Benjamin: "How can a pure man keep his way pure?
By guarding it according to thy word."

> *For Abigail: "Teach [her] good judgment and knowledge,*
> *For [she] believes in thy commandments."*
> *For Levi: "Let thy steadfast love come to [him],*
> *O Lord, thy salvation according to thy promise."*

Several hours later, she heard footsteps and looked down to see Abigail staring up at her and realized that the light flooding her room was now sunlight. Leah was amazed at the amount of thread she had been able to spin and overjoyed with the time she had spent with her Heavenly Father in prayer for her family. Her heart was full and she did not feel at all as if she had been deprived of sleep.

She Riseth While it is Still Night

For many years I quickly pointed out my struggle to be a morning person, even while writing this chapter. So you can imagine my temptation to skip this verse, however, as I said earlier, we must add each piece of this passage in order to see the picture.

I discovered a long time ago that one of the things my husband requires from me is my company in the mornings, one of those things I learned from 'listening'. For a long time, I did a very poor job of meeting his need, and I was convinced that my desire for sleep gave me every right to deny him my company in the mornings. There were many mornings when he never saw the whites of my eyes before he left for work. I have since done much better, and take pleasure in providing company and services for my family in the mornings. I have also learned to be very thankful for a husband who enjoys my company.

You will discover, as you begin your journey into meeting your husband's needs, that you may occasionally find yourself taking no pleasure in the task. There were many mornings when I grudgingly crawled out of bed with a much greater desire to sleep. We are going to call these times our difficult seasons. In fact, the Hebrew word for night in proverbs 31:15 is translated as 'season'.

This translation for night is used again in Ruth 3:2 which says, "And now is not Boaz of our kindred with whose maidens thou wast? Behold, he winnoweth barley tonight in the threshing floor." It was customary for the landowner to spend the night near the threshing floor during the threshing season. He would do this in order to protect his grain from theft. Boaz adapted his lifestyle accordingly during this changing and perhaps difficult season.

As wives, we must also be adaptable as we submissively and sacrificially meet our husband's needs, even when we find it to be somewhat difficult. We will have many difficult seasons when it will take every effort we can muster up to lose ourselves and be there for our husbands as God commanded. I can assure you, the chances are great that there will be another woman out there who would be ready and willing, like a thief, to steal your husband and provide his needs. I firmly believe that through our provision as helpmeets, we strengthen our husband's ability to flee from temptation.

Write 1 Corinthians 10:13:

(NIV) The word 'way' in this verse is translated as 'exit'. Where do we find 'exit' signs? We find them over doors, of course. In your ability to be a door between your husband and God, you can help him fight the temptations he may be faced with in the work world where he spends much of his time, whatever that temptation may be. God can use your submissive spirit to bring your husband closer to God each time he flees temptation. Your submission is a big part of that 'exit' sign over the door God will provide for him.

This is another very important reason for you to work long and hard at being a submissive helpmeet for your husband. Like Boaz guarded his grain during the threshing season, you must help guard your husband's heart as you sacrificially offer yourself to him, even in those difficult seasons. Like the women who rose while it was still night, you must attempt to keep that door open at all times, because his relationship with God is the ultimate key to his ability to flee temptation and live a Godly life.

How often has your husband walked in at the end of the day, only to have you hit him in the face with your difficult day? If you want him to care about your seasons, you must first care about his. You cannot listen for his needs if you are always talking about yours.

We cannot allow our own difficulties to close our door or to hide our exit signs. Do you remember the golden rule you learned as a child?

Write Matthew 7:12:

The Greek word for 'do in this verse is a root word translated as 'to rise'. Some of the translations 'do' and 'riseth' have in common are to perform and make good. The word 'riseth' is translated to succeed. The word 'do' is translated as work or yield. The word 'everything' is translated as all things and refers to a *'daily necessity'*. This woman daily sacrificed some sleep in order to make sure her household was properly fed. She was abiding in love, and making good the needs of her family. As she rose each day, she once again yielded herself and treated her family the way we would all like to be loved and treated.

What are you sacrificing daily for your husband and family?

Where do you think you may need to sacrifice daily for your family?

Pray that God will show you now where you have difficult seasons, or times when you are placing your needs above those of your husband and family.

Let's write Matthew 10:39 this way:

> "…And (she) that loses (her) life
> (In the difficult seasons) for my
> Sake shall find it.

7

*D*iscerning *H*earts

She Considereth a field and buyeth it;
With the fruit of her hands she planteth a
Vineyard. Proverbs 31:16

*L*eah turned to see Benjamin standing at the door with a very strange smile on his face. "Look toward the window," he said, "And don't turn around until I tell you." Leah did as he said but with confused reservations. "Okay," said Benjamin, "You may turn around." Leah squealed with delight as she turned back around. It was the crib basket she had seen at the lake front village by the sea. Benjamin laughed with such delight at her look of confusion. He grabbed her hand and pulled her toward him so that she could see this wasn't a dream. "How?" asked Leah. "Sarah's father told me how you planned to buy the basket on your shopping trip with them, but changed your mind to get the net I needed. I gave him the money he needed to get it for you on his last trip. Leah, my father was right when he said that I could trust you because of your love for God. I know that I do not have to worry about your judgment with family and household affairs. The basket will allow you to do more work when Levi is awake," said Benjamin. "And, I know you will sleep much better if you are not worrying that the blankets around him will keep him safe from harm as he sleeps."

Leah smiled as she walked through the village later that day. Benjamin was at home with the children and she had time for gathering flax. She also had a little money tucked away from the linen threads she had been able to spin during her early mornings. A man and his young son stood in the street with several small lambs. "Afternoon, Madam," said the man as she passed. "Wouldn't you like to buy the last of my lambs?" he asked. Leah stopped and smiled at the soft, white, woolly lambs. She had often wished she had just a few sheep to sheer, just like Lydia, so that she could make wool threads for her customers. "I will not be taking them home, I must sell them today," he said. The man then gave her a price. Did she hear him

41

correctly? The price was not only very low but exactly the amount she had with her. Another man who had been listening moved Leah out of the way and said he would buy them. "I asked the nice lady first," said the man with the lambs. Benjamin wasn't here and she had a decision to make. What would he say if she came home with these little lambs? "I'll even walk them home with you, Madam," said the man. Leah knew the price was a bargain for sure. The sheep would provide much wool for thread, especially as they grew. Lydia had taught her everything she needed to know about caring for them and sheering them for the wool she needed to spin thread. "I'll take them," said Leah with a smile and they herded the sheep to their new home. As she walked, she thought about Benjamin's declaration of trust in her that day. She knew she wanted him to be proud of her, and she knew she didn't want to see that look on his face that made her think she had done him 'evil' and not 'good'.

"You have brought home a treasure," said Benjamin with a smile after listening to Leah's story. "Abigail will soon be able to help you take care of the lambs and she will enjoy them very much. The thread you make will bring good money, Leah. You made a wise decision, not for yourself, but for our family."

The Fruit of Her Hands

Let me begin by saying, the words in Proverbs 31:16 do not call a woman out into real estate. Sorry! This verse is actually referring to this woman's use of good judgment.

I have heard women take this verse and try to use it to promote a woman's independence. As we continue the study of this passage, you will discover the freedom that comes in following this wonderful plan God set forth for us as women, but, never will you find any scripture that gives you permission to come out from under your husband's authority in order to promote your independence.

Let's look back at Proverb's 31:11. Remember, "The heart of her husband doth safely trust in her,". Because of what we learned in chapter 2, we know that one of two things took place here. Either she had already consulted her husband about this deal, or she knew, without a doubt, that her husband would approve.

I strongly believe the good judgment this woman used included what I call a *heart attitude of submission*. How many times have you done something without your husband's approval or even without his knowledge? Or perhaps you asked him for something and you knew from his answer, that even though he didn't say no, you were well aware of his disapproval.

We must make decisions daily that require discernment and the use of a heart attitude of submission. The word considereth is translated in a way that leads us to believe she happened upon this field one day. That field we happen upon could be anything from that bargain we find in unfamiliar territory while shopping, or a major decision concerning the children.

I have many friends whose husbands must travel a great deal with their work, and these ladies struggle with this much more than the rest of us. The key here is how well you are using those keen senses and radar as you become more and more discerning of your husband's needs.

I believe that in most situations we will know exactly what decisions our husbands would have us make. You cannot use his absence as an excuse to forget your call of submission. Ephesians 5:24 says "..., so let the wives be [subject] to their own husbands in **everything**." You must carry him with you in your heart and consult his feelings as if he were standing right next to you.

I believe this kind of submission is often the most difficult. It requires doing or not doing based on what you know would be your husband's response if he were present. I also believe it is through a heart attitude of submission that you will discover the greatest blessings in your marriage and in your relationship with God. Every decision you make from a heart attitude of submission will either do your husband good or evil. There is no in-between. If you make decisions based on your needs without your husband's approval, then you do him evil.

Hebrews 5:14 says, "But strong meat belongeth to them that are of full age, even those who by reason of use have their senses exercised to discern both good and evil." The strong meat in this verse refers to our maturity as Christians. Mature, Godly character is developed in those decisions we make through a heart attitude of submission. So, how do we exercise our senses as this verse in Hebrews refers?

Write Hebrews 4:12:

What is the first step toward exercising the 'keen senses' needed for a heart attitude of submission?

To exercise your senses, you must daily turn to God's word. As his word becomes a part of you, it will clearly reveal your heart attitude as you struggle with the decisions you must make. That built in radar and keen senses system God gave us requires this daily exercise if it is to work effectively for our benefit.

The word hands in Proverbs 31:16 is also representative of the closed hands, offering submission, and the relinquishing of power that might lead you to serve yourself in your decision making process.. The fruit of her hands refers to her rewards, the rewards of good judgment.

Proverbs 24:30-31 refers to the sluggard or lazy man and says, "I went past the field of the sluggard, past the vineyard of the man who lacks judgment; thorns had come up everywhere, the ground was covered with weeds, and the stone wall was in ruins."[NIV] The sluggard's use of poor judgment and refusal to care for his vineyard led to *no* rewards. His desires were not met.

Women, who use good judgment, when practicing a heart attitude of submission, are caring for their marriages by removing the thorns and weeds that grow when we refuse submission. When you use poor judgment, you hurt your husband and marriage with the thorns and weeds you leave behind. If you have ever done any gardening, you know that weeds are much more easily removed when they first appear. Leave them, and they grow out of control, often smothering the good fruit and vegetables. There is little reward from a garden like this. Keep it weeded and cared for, and the rewards will be great.

Learn to use good judgment through a heart attitude of submission and you will rarely find your husband questioning the decisions you make. He will know that you are carrying him in your heart.

The sluggard not only lost the rewards of his vineyard, but verse 31 says "...and the stone wall was in ruins." Stone walls or hedges were usually placed around the vineyards to protect them from thirsty animals or thieves. The sluggard's lack of care to his vineyard resulted in the ruin of the wall that served to protect it.

Just as submission in the difficult seasons serves to protect your marriage, so does the heart attitude of submission. Submission is truly the cornerstone of the wall that God is building around your marriage. The harder you work at this calling, the stronger your marriage, and the greater the rewards.

Begin a list of areas in your marriage where you struggle with a 'heart' attitude of submission: What can you do to improve these areas?

Each time you are obedient to God, through submission and obedience to your husband, you are adding another stone to your wall of protection as you strengthen and keep it from ruin. Do I hear an AMEN?

Let's write Matthew 10:39 this way.

> "...and [she] that loseth [her] life
> (By using a heart attitude of submission)
> For my sake shall find it.

8

---

*E*ffective *A*ctions

She girdeth her loins with strength
And strengtheneth her arms. Proverbs 31:17

L eah watched out the window as Benjamin played with Abigail and Levi. Leah's friend, Sarah, had stopped outside and was talking with Benjamin. As Benjamin smiled at Sarah, Leah remembered the way he used to smile at her when they walked through the village. Her heart began to pound and she wondered if Benjamin had really hoped to marry Sarah. Why hadn't his father chosen Sarah? Everyone thought she was the most beautiful girl in the village. Sarah had not hidden her disappointment when she became betrothed to Jacob and it had not been a good marriage. Sarah had been such a good friend and Leah had not felt these waves of jealousy until now. Benjamin motioned for Leah to come outside as he glanced at the window and saw her standing there. "Leah, you are the luckiest girl in the village," Sarah said. "You have such a beautiful, special family." Leah smiled at her and wondered if Sarah was in love with Benjamin. Leah wondered why she was thinking about all of this now. Benjamin had never given her any reason to believe he wanted someone else or that he was unhappy with her in any way. Why was her mind flooded with these thoughts now? They visited for awhile and Leah noticed that Sarah rarely took her eyes off Benjamin.

The next day, Leah found it very difficult to concentrate on her work. Why couldn't she stop these anxious thoughts from flooding her mind? Suddenly she began singing Psalms 147:

> "Praise the Lord…For He strengthens the bars of your gates;
> …He makes peace in your borders…"

Leah sang these words over and over again until she realized that she no longer felt anxious. Leah remembered the apostle Paul had talked about the importance of girding up the loins of your mind. She had thought it was one of the strangest things she had ever heard, but now it became very clear to her. He had said it was very important to think about things that are Godly in order to keep your mind clear of anxious thoughts. She was experiencing her very own battle, created in her mind, and God just wanted her to trust Him to strengthen the gates around her family and grant peace to her borders. Focusing on these disturbing thoughts might take her mind in other directions and she realized she might just be fighting a battle that existed in her mind only. Leah knew that she didn't like these thoughts because they gave her feelings of helplessness and entrapment. She preferred the feelings of freedom that came when she placed everything at Christ's feet and trusted God to protect her. Leah would pray every morning for God to strengthen the gates around her family and to grant peace to their borders. This would be her way of girding the loins of her mind spiritually as she literally girded her loins physically to work in service for Benjamin and her family. God would take care of the rest!

Leah looked up to see Benjamin smiling at her. "We should all go to the prayer gathering tonight, Leah," he said. Her heart pounded with joy because it had been so long since they worshipped together. She smiled as she felt the rush of 'peace' within her borders.

She girdeth her loins

To gird one's loins refers to the tucking of the loose ends of clothing into a belt or armor of some type. This gesture was representative of some type of action about to take place, perhaps running, battle, or vigorous work.

The word girdeth is translated 'to put on'. The word strength is translated as boldness, force, and security. We have already seen that the word virtuous is translated as a force.

I believe the phrase in Proverbs 31:17 refers to this woman's desire to put her time to good use by working vigorously at her tasks. Girding her loins represents her refusal to allow any unnecessary distractions. Her enthusiasm and vigor in putting away distractions served as her strength for getting things done.

When was the last time you felt as if you had all the time you had needed at the end of the day? If your answer is anything like mine, it would be never.

As I am writing this, I am also looking outside at our one and a half acre lawn that I offered to mow for my husband. At the other end of the room is a sink full of dishes that cannot be loaded into the dishwasher until it has been unloaded. In my bedroom is a stack of clothes to be ironed that could literally take hours. I pick up my daughter from school at 2:30. I have a student coming for tutoring at 3:00, ladies quartet practice at 4:30, and somewhere in there I will need to prepare dinner. Sound like a normal day for you?

I love sharing scripture with you, and another of my favorites is on a shelf behind me. It says "My times are in thy hands...," Psalm 31:15. In order to use our time wisely, we must begin by acknowledging God as the author and creator of our times.

As we gird up our loins with strength, we must first draw on the strength of God as we begin our daily times with Him. 1 Peter 1:13 says, "Wherefore gird up the loins of your mind, be sober, and hope to the end for the grace that is to be brought unto you at the revelation of Jesus Christ." This refers to putting away distractions in your mind. The use of our time physically must begin spiritually in our minds if we are to produce effective actions.

The word strengthen, in Proverbs 31:17, is translated as to be alert physically or mentally, to be courageous or steadfastly minded. The translation for arms in this verse refers to the out stretched arm as it is ready for action.

Whatever a day provides or brings our way is directly from God. How we handle, use, or go about our times is up to us. We can again choose to serve ourselves with the daily choices we make or the unnecessary distractions we allow into our homes and hearts, or we can choose to serve God through service to our family. We must gird up our loins with the strength of the Lord if we are to make the best of our days.

Paul gave us some wonderful words of advice for girding our loins spiritually and strengthening our minds.

Write Philippians 4:8:

Circle the things Paul says we should do to strengthen our minds:

Paul is exhorting us and reminding us that what we are and what we do begins in our minds. We are what we think!

What type of music do you listen to? Does it follow Paul's advice?

What type of television shows do you watch?

What are your friends involved with? Do they follow Paul's advice?

How could any of these things keep you from girding up the loins of your mind?

When we allow ungodly distractions into our minds and into our homes, we are not caring for them as God desires. When men went into battle, they also girded up their loins into the armor they wore. In this way, their clothing was not a distraction as they fought, which gave them the strength of freedom. Satan is intent on destroying our marriages and families. We are daily at battle to protect them. Here we find yet another precious way to provide that strength needed in the walls of protection around our families.

1 John 4:4 says "...greater is he that is in you than he that is in the world." The only way that Satan can defeat you is if you allow him the opportunity. Your salvation has provided you with the strength to defeat Satan and keep him from destroying the marriage God ordained for you. But, it takes work. Not just the physical work required, but most importantly, the work that begins in your mind. You must be steadfast and follow Paul's advice. Every ungodly distraction you allow into your mind or in your home serves to ruin that wall of protection around a fruitful marriage and family.

Begin a list of things that you feel might be 'distractions' in your day as a wife, mother, etc.:

Pray fervently that God will give you the strength to let go of those ungodly distractions that are tripping you and keeping you from using your time wisely. Pray for strength to keep your mind on those things that are Godly. I have learned to keep my television off or it will certainly lure me into its addictive power of idleness. I keep my radio on a Christian station or play Christian music as I work at home or travel in my car. These are ways I have learned to gird my loins and put away ungodly distractions. There is freedom in this as you are provided with more time for things that are important. You will also find that God will, again, reward your efforts as he provides the strength necessary to do all that you need to do in that 'never-ending' day.

Let's write Matthew 10:39 this way.

...and [she] that loses [her] life
[By putting away ungodly distractions]
For my sake shall find it.

9

Illuminated Doors

She perceiveth that her merchandise is good.
Her candle goeth not out by night. Proverbs 31:18

"O h, taste and see that the Lord is good;

Blessed is the [one] that trusteth in him."

Leah sang the words from Psalm 34 with new passion and ownership as she gathered the piles of woolly fibers she had just sheered. Leah tasted the life possible for the woman who was willing to accept her unique purpose in 'The Kingdom'. God had blessed her decision to purchase the lambs and her wool threads had brought in much more profit than they had hoped. Leah and Benjamin had been able to trade for a loom and she was now able to weave her beautiful linen and wool threads into cloth. Leah had also learned how to weave the flax stalks and fibers into baskets. Leah had been amazed at how much more she was able to accomplish as the children grew. She was also amazed at how they always had exactly what they needed.

Leah smiled as she listened to Abigail and Levi singing the 'scriptures' she had taught them. She was so thankful that God had supplied such a wonderful way for her children to learn and remember the scriptures and she loved listening to them sing. Abigail would often sit with Levi and teach him the 'scripture' songs while Leah worked.

"Let's make a new song," Levi squealed to Abigail. Leah beamed as she listened to Abigail sing:

"Praise the Lord!
Sing to the Lord a new song;
His praise in the assembly of the faithful."

49

"That is from Psalms 149, Levi," said Abigail. The two continued to sing the song and soon Leah was singing along with them. Benjamin walked in with a surprised look on his face. "Did your mother teach you a new song today?" he asked. "No, father," said Abigail. "God gave me a new song." Soon, they were all singing Abigail's song of praise. Leah saw the look of pride and joy in Benjamin's face as he sang.

"Oh, taste and see that the Lord is good," Leah thought as she watched her family!

The Taste is good!

I am so excited and anxious to show you where we have come at this point. If you have ever put together a jigsaw puzzle, you know it is much easier to first find all of your border pieces and form the outer frame for your picture. Well, that is exactly what we have done. The picture will slowly, but surely form before your eyes as we bring it to completion.

You see, I believe that is what is happening in this verse. This woman has begun to see the picture and she is anxious to bring it to completion. Not only that, but she likes what she is seeing. This woman is excited! Why? Because, she has, with the selfless, serving spirit of Ruth, come to accept the purpose in her creation. She has learned to lose herself as she accepts her place in the chain of command and her calling of submission. She has learned to exercise and effectively use her keen senses. She has learned how to gird up her loins with strength to produce effective actions and use her time wisely. She has learned that she is strengthening and protecting her marriage and family.

Have you figured out where I am going with this? This woman, in losing herself, has already begun to find herself, and she is thrilled at what she is finding. Remember, the word virtuous is taken from a Hebrew root which means 'standing proudly in the midst of battle.' This woman is standing proudly because she is discovering how to win the battles by following God's plan for her life.

The word perceiveth in Proverbs 31:18 is translated 'to taste'. The word merchandise is synonymous with trading and is translated 'profit'. I believe the trading that took place in this verse was the trading of good for evil, the trading of an ungodly life for a Godly life within the boundaries set forth for us in scripture. She has literally traded herself and her own selfish desires for a life of service for God and her family. She is realizing the profit or rewards of her trading. She is finding herself and it 'tastes' good. Do you have chill bumps yet? I did as I wrote this.

I believe that if this woman had access to David's writing, she may have been sitting back reading Psalm 34. Let me show you what verse 8 of this psalm says. "O taste and see that the Lord is good; blessed is the man [or woman] that trusteth in him." The word taste in this verse is the exact same Hebrew translation we see in Proverbs 31:18. This Psalm absolutely sums up what this verse in Proverbs is saying. Blessed or profitable is the woman who trusts and lives by my word. The taste is good.

How do we know she is anxious to bring her picture to completion? Proverbs 31:18 also says "... her candle goeth not out by night." She has begun to realize that the work involved in her calling leaves no place for idleness. The word night is the same translation we found in Proverbs 31:15. It means 'season'. She is now ready and willing to go all out, never letting her lamp burn down. She is on call for her husband and her family at all times, in all seasons. She is available for her family in every way, at any time.

What benefits have you begun to see at this point in your study?

(If you are not able to see benefits at his time, I would suggest you go back through the first part of this study again to see where you might be struggling or perhaps need to be more patient.)

Which part of God's design for marriage do you struggle with the most? Why?

Write a prayer here and begin praying each day that God will help you lose yourself in this area:

We have shown how a woman, who lives according to these boundaries set forth by God in scripture, is comparable to a door between her husband and God. This woman has learned how to open her door and keep it open. Not only that, but she is going to keep a light in it at all times. In Matthew 5:15-16, Jesus said "Neither do people light a lamp and put it under a bowl. Instead they put it on its stand and it gives light to everyone in the house...".[NIV] She is placing her light on the stand, by her open door with every intention of keeping it burning. I believe some of the good profit she might have tasted was her husband's ability to see God when her door is open and her lamp is lit. Her good and Godly lifestyle began to allow her husband to see, and perhaps praise her heavenly father. This would be another reason for her to be anxious to continue her good deeds and complete the picture by keeping her lamp burning.

Her continuous burning lamp is the love her husband and family see in her for God, and for them, as she serves them in obedience and with joy. Her relationship with God has become inviting to her family.

Let's write Matthew 10:39 this way.

> "...and [she] that loses [her] life
> [By keeping her lamp burning]
> For my sake shall find it.

Remember, a lighted doorway is so much easier to find, and bids a welcomed entrance.

10

*S*uccessful *C*ycles

She stretches out her hands to the distaff
And her hands grasp the spindle. Proverbs 31:19

Leah's eyes became very heavy as she sat at the spinning wheel, but she jumped when she felt Benjamin's hand on her shoulder. "Come back to bed with me, darling," he said gently. Leah looked at the spindle of thread in front of her. It was almost finished, but she rose from her stool and smiled at Benjamin. She knew from the look on his face that he desired to be with her.

Leah awoke hours later as sunlight flooded the room. She was alarmed by the quiet. Leah was very aware of how rested she felt as she walked around their empty home. Where was the family? Leah sat and quickly finished the spool of thread she had struggled to complete earlier that morning.

Leah rose from the spinning wheel in time to see her family coming through the door. "Father took us out in the boat," said Levi excitedly. "We watched him catch some fish." Abigail excitedly told her mother about singing in the boat. "We couldn't sing until we were finished fishing, Mother," said Abigail, "Or the fish would swim away."

"I knew you needed to rest this morning," Benjamin said lovingly as he looked into Leah's eyes. "You have been working very hard, Leah, and I will help with the children today. Abigail is determined to prepare our meal and I will help her."

Leah looked at the spool of thread in her hand and her eyes moved to watch her family. She felt surrounded by love as she observed the love on the faces of her husband and children as they prepared the meal. Leah had been spinning beautiful thread for years, but she suddenly realized she had been spinning more than just thread. The spool of thread in her hand was the product of hard work, but the love and laughter that filled her home right now was the product of a different kind of work.

Open Hands

Let me begin by giving you a picture of the woman as she spins thread. Her left hand holds the distaff. The distaff also holds the wool or flax fibers. It prepares or makes ready the fibers for spinning. With her right hand, she uses her fingers to draw the fleece and form it into thread as it is wound around the spindle. The spindle is turned with the thumb of the right hand as it swings away in circles.

We have already looked carefully at her working hands in chapter 4. We saw her work as a submissive, sacrificial offering of herself. In chapters 6 and 9, we see her willingness to keep her candle burning and work into the night or rise early as she offers herself in service to her family.

What we see here in this verse is a very accurate description of her never-ending work. Her work is a continual cycle. She is willing to work hard and around the clock. I believe a very contemporary translation for this verse could be 'a woman's work is never done.' Amen?!

The words 'stretches out' are translated as layeth in the KJV. This translation means to send away, give over, cast out or dismiss. It indicates a completed action. This is another indication of her sacrifice as she gives over her hands in sacrifice for her family. She is casting out herself. She is dismissing and sending away idleness. She is sending it away as she tightly grasps her work. The completed success on her spindle is there because of her willingness to work hard. The success on her spindle is original. She will never come back to this particular cycle again. If she had chosen to put away this particular cycle, the success on her spindle would be lost forever. Her work for her family is the basis for her life. It is never-ending and it is here where she finds her success. Her cycles of work will produce and yield the needs of her family. She realizes the necessity of putting away idleness as the key to more and greater successes.

Ecclesiastes 11:6 says, "Sow your seed in the morning and at evening let not your hands be idle, for you do not know which will succeed..." Your work will yield many successes. Some will be tangible and others intangible.

The spindle 'holds' the finished product of her work. She holds or grasps it in her hand. Hold is also translated as attain. She has attained the success that comes from hard work. Proverbs 31:19 uses the 'closed' hand translation offering submission, but we also see the other Hebrew translation for 'hands'. This translation refers to an 'open' hand which represents the success and rest that come at the end of every cycle she completes. The 'open' hand is a direct result of a cycle that begins with 'closed', submissive hands. The 'open' hand is full of success for others and for her. It is not possible in a cycle that doesn't begin with 'closed' hands.

Our refusal to be idle will certainly bring success into our homes. Some days that success may be no more than the smiles on the faces of your family as they see your love represented in all you have done for them. When that frightened or sick child screams for you in the middle of the night, those resting hands must go to work as you hold and care for that child. Your success is the love and comfort that child feels from your presence. When your husband reaches for you in the middle of the night, those resting hands must once again go to work as you hold him close. The greatest success of your day may be found here, rather than in your morning's physical labor. When was the last time you dropped to your knees and lifted those hands in petition as an intercessor for your husband and children? 1 Thessalonians 5:17 says, "pray without ceasing." This means continually, permanently, without omission. There is no room for idleness in our prayer life.

When was the last time you met your family's needs by spending time with them at *their* request?

This work is just as important as those physical needs we meet on a daily basis. What kind of balance are you providing for your family?

We saw at the beginning of this study that the virtuous woman in Proverbs is being compared to wisdom. Go back to the picture of this woman spinning her thread. Make a mental note of how she is using her hands. Now let's read Proverbs 3:16. "Long life is in her right hand; in her left hand are riches and honor." This verse is referring to wisdom, but, it accurately describes the success she holds in her hands as she sacrificially offers them for her family. Also, we see another indication of the power referred to in the translation of hands. By relinquishing herself, she is offering the power possible as God blesses her hard work and effort.

Her hard, continuous work offered the riches and honor God gives to those who have learned to fear him and trust him. The long life she holds in her right hand represents the ultimate power possible from a life of righteousness. It is important to note that what we see here is a woman's ability to be used by God to provide material blessings for her family. However, this is not her main goal. It is not a result of her, but rather a result of what she is *willing to do* for God and for her family.

> 'But seek *first* his kingdom and
> His righteousness and all these
> Things will be given to you as well.
> Matthew 6:33 [NIV]

So, what about that time of rest? Is there really any rest for the weary?

Write Philippians 4:19:

Which needs will God supply for us?

According to what?

God did not give you a calling that he did not intend to help you with. He will certainly hear your weary cries for rest. Your success is dependent on the strength you draw from a time of rest. Your time for open, resting hands will come.

Let's write Matthew 10:39 this way.

> "...and [she] that loses [her] life
> [With her never ending *cycles* of work]
> For my sake shall find it.
> (And her greatest success)

Meeting His Needs Emotionally

Emotional Separation

We have seen how the virtuous woman was submissive to her husband. She was willingly submissive, even during the difficult seasons. She also had a heart attitude of submission by consulting his feelings even when he was not present. What we have discovered in chapters 4-7 is that submission is the basis for meeting our husband's needs emotionally.

I want us to read The Song Of Solomon, 5:2-6.

"I slept but my heart was awake. Listen! My lover is knocking; open to me, my sister, my darling, my dove, my flawless one. My head is drenched with dew, my hair with the dampness of the night. I have taken off my robe-must I put it on again? I have washed my feet-must I soil them again? My lover thrust his hand through the latch opening; my heart began to pound for him. I arose to open for my lover, I opened for my lover, but my lover had left, he was gone. My heart sank at his departure. I looked for him but did not find him. I called him but he did not answer,"

The Lord confused me at first, by leading me to this passage for emotional needs, but I quickly discovered his reasons. When this woman's lover came to her, she whined and offered him flimsy excuses, rather than offering him submission. She didn't want to put her robe back on or get her feet dirty. However, when she discovered her own desire for him was present, she got up to let him in, but he was gone. Most commentators of this passage agree that what we see here is an example of the emotional separation that occurs when we refuse to meet each other's needs. Not just physical needs, but any need falling under the mental, emotional or spiritual needs categories.

Let's go back to Genesis 3:16. Part of the judgment on the woman after her sin was that "...your desire will be for your husband..." The Hebrew word for desire is teshuvqah [tesh-oo-kaw]. It means stretching out after, or a longing for. It is from a root word meaning to run after or over, also to overflow as water.

God's judgment on the woman placed us not only under our husband's authority, but also promised trouble and anguish as we long for them. I am convinced that every woman has an area in her relationship with her husband where she is longing for more of him either physically, emotionally, or spiritually. God had originally placed the woman by the man's side with everything she needed. Her sin took him away from her as he left her side to toil and labor in the workplace. We are destined to miss them, and always feel we need more from them. They are destined to feel the constant tug of work on one side and our overflowing longing for them on the other side. No wonder most men are so stressed out.

In the Song of Solomon, we see the man basically disappear from the scene once she says that he has departed. Isn't that just like a man? Upset him and he retreats into himself without a word. The woman, however, goes emotionally crazy. We see in the rest of this chapter and the next, she is overflowing with longing, but she can't reach him. Her refusal to offer submission has driven him away. She has lost that moment with him.

Oh, how often we do this to our husbands. They come to us with a need, and we shoot back with excuses. Then we throw our needs in their face and wonder why they retreat or become angry. Our emotional make-up is a direct result of our judgment.

Emotional separation causes the man to withdraw. Verse six says "...my lover had left; he was gone...I called but he did not answer." Sound familiar? When the man withdraws, it is almost impossible to get him to talk to you. When a man is emotionally withdrawn, it will be almost impossible for him to respond to your cries of need.

Emotional separation causes the woman to feel abandoned. In verse six she says "...I looked for him but I did not find him..." He may be there physically, but emotionally he has removed himself from what he sees as a no win situation.

The woman will verbally accuse her husband of not being there for her. He will be thinking that she never wants to be there for him. Emotional separation is traumatic for husband and wife, but can be avoided when the wife respectfully meets her husband with submission and not with flimsy excuses.

Submission is the key to keeping your husband emotionally content. And, I am convinced that when we meet them with respect and submission, they will be more likely to meet us where we are and listen to our needs.

Emotional Stability

Every woman wants to be loved and feel needed by her husband. In our destiny to long for this we are offered hope, and that hope lies in our ultimate desire for God.

> "Delight yourself in the Lord and
> He will give you the desires of your heart.
> Commit your ways unto the Lord, trust in
> Him; and he will do this."

God says desire me above everything, even your husband, and I will make your longings and desires a part of your life. Amen!

God can and will work in your husband's life and give him the desire to meet your needs as you respond to your husband's needs through submission. As your desire for God grows, you will discover how much easier it is to follow your calling of submission. You will become more comfortable with this calling and you will also discover the blessings that follow. I am convinced that God desires to give us a 'taste' of the garden. You will discover how to find that 'taste' as we continue our study. I assure you, it can only happen by following this design from beginning to end.

Part Three

Meeting His Needs Physically

11

*P*ortable *L*amps

She stretcheth out her hand to the poor;
Yea she reaches forth her hands to the needy.
Proverbs 31:20

Leah realized that her work as a wife and mother was providing for more than just physical needs as she discovered how emotionally and spiritually connected they were growing as a family. She knew it was time for her to begin teaching Abigail how to reach out to others. Leah's friend, Sarah, had been ill and today Leah and Abigail would take her some food and visit for awhile.

Leah always enjoyed Sarah's outgoing spirit of fun. Leah often wished she could be more like Sarah in that way. Today, however, was much different. Sarah's smile was obviously forced and her infectious laugh was nowhere to be found today. Leah was horrified when she saw Sarah and certainly felt unprepared for what she discovered. The most difficult part of this visit was trying to find ways to cheer Sarah and take her mind off the situation. Sarah's eyes would sparkle only when watching Abigail and listening to tales about Levi. Sarah said very little, but kept reminding me, "Leah, God has blessed you with Benjamin. Never take him for granted."

The travel back home was also difficult as she attempted to answer Abigail's questions about Sarah. "Mommy," asked Abigail, "why did Mrs. Sarah have bruises on her face?" "Mommy doesn't know, Abigail," I said. "Maybe she fell, Mommy!" urged Abigail. "Yes, Mommy, I'm sure that is what happened!" "Maybe so," said Leah, "Maybe so."

Portable lamps

Can you remember the last time you were without electricity? Did you find yourself carrying oil lamps and candles around with you, and placing them in the darkest areas of your home? There are so many things we would never attempt to do without sufficient light. Success would be almost impossible.

We live in a world of darkness. Ecclesiastes 2:13-14 says,"…light excels darkness…, but the fool walks in darkness." There are so many in this world choosing to walk in darkness. They live their lives in confusion, frustration, and unnecessary depression. As a child of the king, we have a portable lamp, and God has commanded that we offer this light to those around us who are living in darkness.

This woman is willing to go beyond her world and her comfort zone in order to reach out to others. She is willing to give of herself physically, mentally, emotionally, and spiritually if necessary. She is willing to share her profit and the fruit of her labor.

Do you remember Matthew 5:15? "Neither do people light a lamp and put it under a bowl. Instead they put it on its stand, and it gives light to everyone in the house." [NIV] Let's add verse 16. "In the same way, let your light shine before men that they may see your good deeds and praise your Heavenly Father in heaven." [NIV] Jesus' words are commanding us to first shine our light at home. Please, keep your lamp burning at all times, because our burning lamp can lead our families through the door into God's arms. He also commands us not to forget that there are others in this world in need of God's loving arms. Our willingness to meet their needs is our way of shining that light that could lead them directly into His arms. Our portable lamps can allow us the opportunity to share, and reflect God to the rest of the world.

You can start with your neighborhood to discover needs or perhaps your church has a women's ministry that provides opportunities for this kind of service. There may even be some community groups available that would allow you the opportunity to share yourself with others. Perhaps God is calling you to start an area of ministry in your church or community that would allow a way for you to shine the light of Jesus Christ in the path of those who need Him. Use your keen senses and radar as you watch and listen for those in need. This woman was shining her light before men long before Jesus issued the command.

I think it is important to point out that this woman, in the last eleven verses, has cared for her husband and family. We have only one verse in Proverbs 31 that shares her commitment to others. This confirms to us that our families' needs should take precedence. Why? They are our God-given responsibility. Their eternal destiny and ability to live godly lives is our main reason for shining our light at home. However, we should not use our families as an excuse to avoid sharing our lamps where God has called. When God does call, we are to trust that His provisions for our family will be sufficient. Therefore, we will at times need to trust Him to watch over them while we step out to shine His light into the world around us.

In Proverbs 31:20, we see the 'open' and 'closed' translations for the word hand. This very clearly shows her willingness and availability to God. She is willing to offer whatever the need may be as she shines that light.

The closed hand she offers reveals her willingness to offer labor and service away from home as she offers all she is and can be. The closed hand reveals a servant's heart, submissive to God, and his call to serve others in obedience to him. That woman, today, might clean a home for someone in need. She might volunteer her time for a worthy cause or sit and listen to someone who is hurting. That woman today might work away from the home where she is helping to meet her family's financial needs and also shining her light for those who work alongside of her. She might teach a class at church.

The open hand offers the fruits of her labor and hard work. It reveals her willingness to perhaps sacrifice and share her gain with others in need. The open hand reveals an unselfish heart. This woman, with her outstretched, open hand, offers gifts. That woman, today, might provide meals for those in need. She might provide money for others going on mission trips.

What are some ways that you could shine your light to others away from your home?

Many women worry that working outside the home will prevent them from adequately providing for their families. If you are certain that your job is a calling from God, then you need not worry. He will provide all that you and your family need to function within that calling as you use that place of work to shine your light before others.

If God calls you out to share your portable lamp, you can be sure someone in need of that light will be watching. Praise God! Read what Oswald Chamber said in <u>My Utmost for His Highest: (6)</u>

> "You can never give another person that which you have found,
> But you can make him homesick for what you have."

Our hands should be stretching and reaching our light out to others so brightly and willingly that we make them homesick for what we have found in Jesus Christ.

Let's write Matthew 10:39 this way.

> "…and [she] that loseth [her] life
> [By shining her light to those in need]
> For my sake shall find it."

"A generous [woman] will prosper; [she] who refreshes others will [herself] be refreshed." Proverbs 11:25 Amen!

12

*C*rimson *C*lothes

She is not afraid of the snow for her household;
For all her household are clothed in scarlet.
Proverbs 31:21

Abigail could not stop smiling as she slipped on the beautiful purple coat her mother had made. The beautiful scarlet lining made it feel so warm. "Oh, Mommy," said Abigail. "I am ready for winter to come so that I can wear my new coat!" "How long is it until winter, Mommy?" Leah beamed as she watched Abigail dancing around the room in her new coat. It was a little big on her, but should last through two winters at least.

Leah breathed a sigh of relief as she realized she had finally prepared clothing for her entire family and they were ready for the cold. She even had time to make a few things for herself.

"Mommy, why is purple the most beautiful color in the whole world?" asked Abigail. "Well, Abigail, purple is actually a very special color," said Leah. "Purple is the color of royalty and is worn by kings, queens, princes, and princesses." "Oh, Mommy am I a real princess?" asked Abigail. "Yes, Abigail," said Leah, "you are the daughter of a king and His name is Jesus Christ." "One day, those of us that have asked him to come and live in our hearts will go to live with Him in His heavenly kingdom," said Leah. "Mommy, I want Jesus to come and live in my heart!" said Abigail. "How, Mommy? How?"

"Well," said Leah, "Do you understand what it means to be a sinner and live with sin in your life every day?" Abigail thought for a minute and hung her head. "Mommy, is that like when I told you that I didn't push Levi but I really did?" "Yes, Abigail, that is sin and sin is disobedience to God," said Leah. "Sin separates us from God." "The Bible tells us we are all sinners (Romans 3:23) and that we should die forever because of our sin." (Romans 6:23) "Abigail, the Bible also tells us that God loved us, and the world, so *much that He sent his only begotten son, Jesus Christ, and that whosoever believes in Him should not perish (or die) but have everlasting life." (John 3:16)*

"Mommy, you know I do believe in Jesus. I believe he died on the cross like you have always told me. Mommy, how can Jesus live in my heart?" "Abigail," said Leah, "all you need to do is say a prayer and ask Him to come and live in your heart and tell him all the things you just told me." "Mommy, I want to pray that right now and ask Jesus to live in my heart." "Please, Mommy, please!"

Crimson Clothes

This woman did not dread the cold of winter for those in her family. She made sure they were clothed appropriately for warmth. Not only that, but the word scarlet refers to a royal color, which means they not only felt warm, they also looked great!

She cared about the way her family was dressed, but she also went to a lot of trouble to outfit this household. When I prepare to sew, I just get out my fabric, pattern, and notions and in a few hours I have a creation. This woman, on the other hand, spent hours just making thread, and had to weave that thread into fabric. The fabric had to be colored or dyed.

The color scarlet, or crimson, denotes pain and sacrifice. I think the color represented in this verse is very appropriate, because every piece of clothing worn by her family was a sacrifice of love that literally took days or even weeks to make. Can you imagine the pride they must have felt when receiving and wearing such a gift of love? We are finding it much easier today to clothe our families without sitting at the spinning wheel all day, but the force behind this woman's work is the time she is spending to care for her family.

I think it is important for us to continue studying this woman's sacrificial abilities. I'm not sure that many of us would pass the virtuous woman test if we had to make the sacrifices this woman was required to make. No shopping centers or malls! No restaurants or fast food places when she was too tired to cook! No television to sit the children in front of when she needed a break! However did she manage?

Even with all of these conveniences in our lives, we still have filled our lives with so many things that take us away from our families or prevent us from being there for them as we need to be. Our families need this same kind of sacrificial spirit from us today. They need the time and energy we are spending on things God never called us to do. Our selfish search for success and significance has taken us away from our families. God has always intended that our greatest success and feelings of significance come from our obedience to him as we serve Him and our families. I can certainly smell the smoke coming from some of you right now as you read this. If you are angry with my words, then maybe you are feeling guilty because you do not want to be sacrificial for your family.

God has given you a calling of submission and service to your family. He would not call you out to do anything that would interfere with that calling without making provisions that you are totally comfortable with. If you are comfortable with all you are doing and believe you are called, then you need not be angry with my words. Just take comfort in how God is caring for you and your family. If, however, you are living with guilt or in constant confusion over whether you are doing what is best for your family, then you need to stop and pray that He will clear up this picture for you.

I cannot stress to you enough how crucial is the part you play in caring for your husband and family. This entire study is devoted to bringing your life into focus as God has in the past, and does now, intend for you to live. This woman's sacrificial spirit may seem extreme to you, but I say that is exactly the word that best describes our family's need for sacrifice on our part-EXTREME! We were not called to live our lives for ourselves, but in service to God and our families. If you are not happy with that calling, then you need to take it up with God because it is His design for the family!

Pray that God will show you where your needs and desires are keeping you from dressing your family in the crimson clothes of pain, sacrifice, and love. What if this woman had decided it was just too much trouble to make thread and fabric day after day. She would have missed out on the joy of providing more than just clothing for her family. She was providing herself. Scarlet also denotes bloodshed. Jesus Christ made the ultimate crimson sacrifice of death for us. How dare we think we owe Him anything less.

We have the opportunity to offer crimson clothing to our families spiritually as we sacrificially offer ourselves to them daily. The material things you work so hard to provide will not go with them when they leave this world. The crimson clothing you provide spiritually will follow them to heaven.

Write Deuteronomy 11:18-20

How much of God's word is clothing your children? What are they learning about Jesus from you and your life? Is the majority of your energy and time touching them inwardly or outwardly? Provide crimson clothing for your family spiritually, and I tell you there is no greater calling for a woman than this!

"…and [she] that loses [her] life
(In daily sacrifice)
For my sake shall find it. Matthew 10:39
[And her family dressed in the beauty of crimson clothing]

13

*P*ure *C*lothes

She maketh herself coverings of tapestry;
Her clothing is silk and purple. Proverbs 31:22

Benjamin smiled as he walked in and saw Leah and Abigail sitting at the small table in their home. "Daddy!" screamed Abigail. "Mommy is stitching my favorite verse, John 3:16, on some of her linen." "Daddy, it is so beautiful," said Abigail. "I will have it forever."

"Abigail, that is so special," said Benjamin. "It will always remind you of the time you prayed and asked Jesus to come into your heart." "I will put it right on top of my pillow so that I can see it every day," said Abigail. "And, Daddy, look at the beautiful pillow mommy made for your bed. She stitched flowers all over it and I helped," said Abigail. "I saw your mommy working on this for weeks," said Benjamin. "I knew it would look very pretty."

"Leah is that a new tunic you are wearing?" asked Benjamin. Leah wore a beautiful purple tunic. Her head covering of red, white, and purple was attached to the tunic for easy access when needed. The head covering was trimmed with beautiful embroidered flowers. "Daddy," said Abigail, "All the women we saw today wanted Mommy to make them a tunic just like hers." "Yes," said Leah, "I am sure I will be quite busy over the winter months with my sewing." "I am glad that Abigail is old enough to help some because we will be able to do so much more work together."

Leah loved the look of peace and contentment she saw on Benjamin's face. He was beginning to realize that God would bless their hard work and truly provide for their physical needs. Leah was very thankful for her ability to help provide their physical needs and she was especially thankful for her part in putting that look on Benjamin's face. Benjamin's trust in her was evident whenever his eyes looked her way with *this contented gaze. "You should stitch me a sparrow," said Benjamin as he smiled at Leah. Leah smiled back because she knew he was referring to*

Something Jesus had said (Matthew 6:25-27) and his understanding of God's provision in their lives.

Pure clothes

Let me show you the NIV translation for this verse. "She makes coverings for her bed; she is clothed in fine linen and purple." Proverbs 31:22

I feel this is a great place for us to see that even though this woman sacrificially gave of herself in service to her family, she did not neglect herself. She is truly a woman after our own heart. She enjoys decorating and she makes coverings for her bed. This word coverings is translated 'coverlet of tapestry' which means she had great taste!

The word 'decorate' is near and dear to every woman's heart in one way or another. This is one reason why so many of us would admit to an obsession with HGTV. I am thankful for the ability to record my favorite HGTV shows for later viewing or I might never get anything done.

We have already learned a lot about this virtuous woman, and I feel it is safe to say that her decorating began with her family's needs and not as a matter of show. I can still remember a time in my life when I cared more about how my home looked to other people. I was not decorating for my family, but for myself and for others. I believe a home should reflect the personalities of all its members, provide comfort, and above all, the presence of Christ should be felt in every room.

When a home reflects the personalities of all its members, you will see or hear a story behind almost everything displayed in that home. For example, the drapes in your home might reflect your love for colors and beauty. The dozen bookshelves scattered throughout your home might reflect your family's love for reading. That collection of your husband reflects something near to his heart, even though you might prefer it in the garage, attic, or basement. How fair are you with the rest of your family as you decorate your home? Does your husband walk in and see a reflection of him? Do your children see reflections of themselves?

Comfort is especially important in any home. That worn out recliner in front of the television may not be ideal to my taste, but it is home for my husband. I hide the stains and missing buttons with a small quilt or 'coverlet'. Those breakables can easily be stored away while your children are young. Children need room to grow without the fear of restrictions we place on them with our sometimes unrealistic expectations. Do your husband and children sense your love for your home as a restriction on them, or as a place of comfort you are decorating just for them?

Is Jesus Christ visibly evident and present in your home? My husband and I have started a collection of religious prints that we proudly display on our walls. Also, I enjoy cross stitching and have placed stitched scripture verses in every room. Our bookshelves are filled, mostly, with Bibles, books and commentaries about the Bible. My daughter and I enjoy shopping for Noah's Ark pieces to add to our collection. Our music reflects our love for worship and gospel music. God is the creator of our home, and we especially want others to see and feel His presence when they visit.

Titus 2:4-5 says, "…teach the younger women to be …keepers at home…" The translation for keepers is an exhortation for us to be good housekeepers. It is taken from a root word meaning 'family, home, or temple'. This is not referring to your ability to keep an immaculate home, but rather your ability to make a home a temple that reflects God and your family's needs.

This woman also reflected God in her own personal appearance. Proverbs 31:22 also says, "...she is clothed in fine linen and purple." Purple denotes royalty or elegance. This woman was no sloppy dresser. Doesn't it make you feel good to know that even this virtuous woman liked dressing up and feeling good about herself? Our outward appearance often provides a first impression and can tell more about a person than you might realize.

My sweet husband gave me a wonderful compliment recently when he told some friends, "One thing I don't have to worry about is the way Cathy dresses." What he was saying was that his heart trusts in me to dress appropriately without wearing anything that he would consider to be unlady-like or in bad taste. The translation for fine linen in this verse refers to a bleached white fabric. White denotes purity. We should dress in a way that frames a pure heart. The number one goal in our outward appearance should point to, or picture, what is on the inside. It is always very obvious when a woman is trying to bring the wrong kind of attention to herself with her clothing.

This verse brings to mind our pastor's precious wife. We call her Mrs. Betty. She is the epitome of elegance to me. She is a lady in the truest form. Her outward appearance, which is never complete without a smile, is always as close to perfection as one can imagine. I see our pastor's pride as he watches her.

Proverbs 12:4 says, "A wife of noble character is her husband's crown, but a disgraceful wife is like a decay in his bones." Our outward appearance should never disgrace our husband. Submission in this area is just as important as in any other place in our marriage.

I have learned how to dress in the style and comfort I enjoy, without doing anything to displease my husband or cause others to question my motives. It was very rewarding to learn my efforts had not gone unnoticed.

I don't know about you, but I desire to be my husband's crown. Did you know that one translation for crown is to encircle for attack or protection? That word protection keeps popping up. Why? It really is possible! Crown your husband with your noble character and pure clothes, and you continue to provide security in that wall of protection.

Titus 2:4-6 says"...teach the younger women...to be chaste..." The word chaste is translated as 'clean, modest, and pure. It is taken from another Greek word meaning 'blameless, sacred, or most holy.

We are to be chaste and pure for God and our families, and not as a means for impressing others. Whether dressing your home or yourself, purity and holiness should always be your decorating guidelines. Are they?

"...and (she) that loses (her) life
(By dressing her home and herself in pure clothes)
For my sake shall find it. Matthew 10:39
(And the reward of respect)

14

*G*odly *G*ates

Her husband is known in the gates,
When he sitteth among the elders.
Proverbs 31:23

Leah was anxious for Benjamin to come home today. She was still very concerned about Sarah after another visit. She was glad she had gone alone this time when she found Sarah in tears. Sarah was not ready to talk but her depression seemed to lighten as she visited with Leah and she smiled as she listened to stories of Abigail and Levi.

When Benjamin finally walked through the door, he had a strange look on his face. He was looking at Leah in a way he had not done before today. He walked over and took Leah in his arms and held her very tightly. This was very strange because Benjamin was not usually affectionate with Leah in public. Leah smiled as she heard Abigail and Levi giggling behind her. "Benjamin, what is going on?" asked Leah. Benjamin took her hand and led her to a seat.

"I was called to the gates today," said Benjamin. "The elders had questions about my friend Joshua who had been accused of stealing from another fisherman. The elders said they called me because they trusted my judgment above all the other fishermen. Leah, I didn't realize until today that they even knew who I was. They believed everything I told them, and as I rose to leave, they said that I should be proud to have a wife of such noble character. Leah, they prayed a blessing over us, our home, and our children. In the prayer, they asked that God would continue to use us so faithfully as a family. Leah, did you know that people were watching us so carefully?" asked Benjamin. "They even mentioned my cheerful countenance as a result of a happy marriage to such a virtuous wife."

"Benjamin," said Leah, "I hear all the time that the other fishermen look up to you because they notice how well you treat other people. They also notice your integrity in the work you do each day and the way you care for your family. It sounds as if others are watching and listening too." "Benjamin, I am so proud of you!" exclaimed Leah, "And, it is such an honor to be your wife."

Godly Gates

The city walls had gateways that served as entrances into the city. Here at these gates, the elders of the city would gather to hold court. They served as witnesses and judges when decisions were made concerning the people of the city.

We see a good example of this as we go back to the story of Ruth, chapter 4. In verse one we see, "Then went Boaz up to the gate, and sat him down there…" In verse two, "…he took ten men of the elders of the city, and said sit ye down here." In verses nine and ten, he says, "…unto the elders, and unto all the people, ye are witnesses this day…moreover Ruth the Moabitess, the wife of Mahlon, have I purchased to by my wife…that the name of the dead be not cut off from among his brethren and from the gate of this place: ye are witnesses this day." In verse eleven, the elders tell Boaz, "We are witnesses. The Lord make the woman that is come into thine house like Rachel and like Leah, which two did build up the house of Israel: and (Boaz) do thou worthily in Ephratah, and be famous in Bethlehem." Here in verse eleven, the elders are acknowledging the importance of a worthy, virtuous, noble wife as they bless Ruth. They also establish the link between this kind of virtuous wife and a husband who does worthily.

These elders are literally leaders of men. A true leader of men has nothing to do with position. It does, however, have everything to do with Godly character and Godly leadership of other men. To be known at the gates was to be recognized as a Godly leader of men.

In Ruth, chapter 2, we see more of Boaz's character in verse four as he returns from Bethlehem and greeted the harvesters, "The Lord be with you!" These are the words of a Godly man.

One of the greatest blessings in my life has been in watching my husband become a Godly man and leader of other men. He is very humble about any positions he might hold, but finds his greatest joy as a teacher and encourager to others. His leadership doesn't come from a need to be seen or known. It is a direct result of a heart turned to God in service. The woman, who is living and painting the picture we have put together so far, has every right to watch for this type of Godly character in her husband. While we have no guarantees, we have loads of hope.

I believe there are two major reasons for a woman's rebellion toward her husband's authority. One of these reasons has to do with his spiritual condition. If your husband is currently standing far away from that doorway to God, please don't close the door by trying to undermine his spiritual condition or leadership as I once did. Scripture has made provision for your frustration, offering not only advice for you, but also the hope that comes in following this advice.

"Wives in the same way be submissive to
Your own husbands so that, if any of them
Do not believe the word, they may be won
Over without words by the behavior of
Their wives when they see the purity and
Reverence of their wives." 1Peter 3:1-2 (NIV)

The word reverence is the same translation we saw for respect. It refers to her fear of God. Here we see another example of the power found in your submission. The scripture says, "...they may be won..." Please, remember again, there are no guarantees, but loads of hope. But, remember, you must follow this God-breathed design very carefully. Just as your favorite recipe would be useless without every ingredient, so this design is useless without following each step. The most important step is our daily realization of our inability to follow this design on our own.

Live with a desire for your husband to be known at the gates as a Godly leader of men. You are the door and the helpmeet who can lead him to that gate. Let go of your expectations for him. God has a set of expectations that are custom designed for your husband. Try and push yours on him and he will have difficulty seeing God's. "Being confident of this very thing, that he which began a good work in you will perform it until the day of Jesus Christ," Philippians 1:6. If your husband is already a Christian, stop working on him! God has that job under control. Get in a hurry and you will get in God's way. Be patient!

1Peter 3:1-2 refers to your gentle and quiet spirit as the key to that 'open door'. Your expectations for your husband can quickly close that door. You must be willing to move away from arguments, especially about spiritual things. It's going to be more important that he see the love of Christ through your behavior and actions.

> "...and (she) that loses (her) life
> (And her expectations) for my sake
> Shall find it." Matthew 10:39

15

Custom Designed Calling

She maketh fine linen and selleth it,
And delivered girdles unto the merchants.
Proverbs 31:24

Leah watched Abigail as she was stitching one of the beautiful belts they had made. Levi sat on the floor watching them both as they worked. "Let's stop and play a game," said Leah. "Really?" asked Levi. "Can we really play a game?" "Mother," said Abigail, "We need to deliver these girdles to the merchants by morning." "Yes," said Leah, "But we can stop and play for a while." Abigail and Levi smiled. Leah beamed as she watched her children playing and she felt as if she could not be any happier than she was at that moment. Leah thought about how rested she felt from the past few nights of sleep and she knew she could rise early enough to finish the girdles before they were to be delivered. As happy as she felt at this moment, Leah also sighed at the realization of how quickly her children were growing. Levi would begin fishing with Benjamin in just three more years. Leah would come of age for betrothal in two more years. Where had the time gone? She wanted very much to tell them that they were getting a baby brother or sister but she would wait for Benjamin to return home from his trip.

Benjamin had traveled with some other men on his first mission to share the gospel of Christ. Leah had told him, just before he left, that she was expecting another baby. Abigail had become such a help to Leah, that she had suggested to Benjamin that they sell some of their sheep so she could slow down a bit and just concentrate on the linen. The new baby would change everything, including the amount of time she had to do all of her jobs. Abigail could continue to help her with the flax for the linen. Benjamin had told her that God had provided all the sheep and He would provide all that she needed to sheer and make the wool. As she watched her children play, she quietly prayed…

"My heavenly Father, as I look back I remember how you have always provided, even when I struggled to trust. Lord, I trust you now and I know that you will provide all I need to continue as a wife, mother, and seamstress. Father, I pray for you to change my heart if necessary or show Benjamin the way of my calling in our home. I thank you for the strength you promised us in all things and I pray that we will be filled with that strength now. In your precious name I pray! Amen!"

Leah looked up to see Benjamin in the doorway. The children squealed as they ran to greet their father. "Leah," said Benjamin, "Luke has asked to buy most of our sheep for a very generous amount. I told him we would keep enough for you to provide wool for our family, but he will purchase the rest. Leah, the money he offered will help for many months so that you can slow down."

"Why must Mother slow down?" asked Abigail. "Well," said Benjamin, "Things are going to be very different around here. You are going to have a new baby brother or sister."

Custom-Designed Callings

We have already learned all this woman went through to make that fine linen. Not only did she make it for her family and for herself, but she also made this fine linen to sell. The girdles are referring to belts or sashes. These are the belts their loins were girded (tucked) into. She also delivered these to the merchants to be sold. This was her work, she was good at it, and she used her talents to provide some extra income.

Most of us, as women, have worked at some point in our lives at or away from home. We can strongly assume this woman worked at home. Her sewing was done at home and her girdles (belts) were delivered elsewhere to be sold. I believe we can assume that she delivered her linen to the merchants also, or perhaps she sold it from her home.

We are given no particular reason why this woman was earning this extra income. Perhaps it was for her family. It may have been used for the volunteer work we saw her do in chapter eleven. She may have been earning this money to give to her church. What we need to realize is that this verse cannot be used as a command or a reason for a woman to work. In chapter twelve, we looked carefully at the sacrificial spirit of this woman. We looked carefully at the woman's primary calling of helpmeet to her husband and her responsibility to care for him and for her family. I will remind you, again here, that God will never call you to anything if it will interfere with your primary calling. You will find no command in scripture that binds a woman to the home or to work. God loves us enough to provide a freedom that allows Him to call us out of the home or to work. We saw another example of this in her provision for the poor and needy. However, we don't have the right to take advantage of this freedom by ignoring God's original call in our lives.

Many women struggle with the work issue. I cannot say to you that working outside the home is right or wrong. I firmly believe it is a matter of calling. I do believe, however, that many families are suffering because women are working at jobs they were never called into by God. Their lives and their families are a mess! They are angry and defensive about what they do, always complaining about never having enough time. They struggle with guilt because their kids spend most of their time with other caregivers.

Many women are working because they believe it is the only way they will feel significant or successful. I hope that if you are one of these women, perhaps you have begun to see where, or from whom, your real success and significance will come.

Many women are working out of submission to their husbands. They would like very much to be at home caring for their families. Now that you realize this is your primary calling, you can begin praying that God will bring you home. When you have prayed and are certain you have a knowledge of your calling, you can rest in 1 Thessalonians 5:24.

> "Faithful is he who calleth you,
> Who also will do it?"

Wherever God has called you to serve Him, he can and will make sure He has removed all the obstacles to get you there. You must wait patiently and continue to live in submission to your husband.

When my daughter was born, I desperately wanted to quit my teaching job and stay home with her. My husband said no because he felt we would not be able to meet our financial obligations without the income I was providing. So, I prayed, knowing that God could and would change my husband's heart and provide the answers we needed financially. He did!

There is a beautiful story in scripture about a woman who was given a very special calling. Her name was Mary, and she was told her calling would be, as a virgin, to give birth to our savior, Jesus Christ. What a calling! Do you remember the first response of her betrothed, Joseph?

What was Joseph's response to Mary's God-given calling in Matthew1: 19?

This was a very loving gesture, with loving intentions, but the wrong response. The earthly father of Jesus was just as human as your husband and mine, thinking logically the way a man does. This is another good reason for us to leave them alone and let God work on them. He made them and he knows how they think. In verse twenty, the lord appeared to Joseph in a dream and set him straight. He would not let Joseph be an obstacle in Mary's calling.

Write Matthew 1:20

God cares just as much about your calling, whatever it may be. He will, if you will trust him enough to ask, remove the obstacles in your way.

We have seen the translation for 'season' throughout this passage in Proverbs 31. I think we need to stop and consider the fact that this passage in proverbs was intended to be a picture for women of all ages. I believe that this passage will take a woman through every season of her life. In fact, I strongly believe that your present season of life will determine God's calling for you during that season. When you become a wife, you immediately receive the calling of helpmeet. When you have children, you immediately receive the calling of mother. Both are fulltime jobs! Amen? Again, God will not call you into something that will take you away from these jobs or would interfere with them on a regular basis. Why would God, who loves you so much, give you two fulltime jobs and then take you away from them? He won't! I can assure you of that.

My daughter was in the first grade when I initially wrote this study. She is now a sophomore in college. I have already been through many seasons in my life, and my 'jobs' have been custom-designed for each season. When I wrote this study, I was at home because God (not me) had changed Mark's heart and taught us both to trust in His provision for us as parents. God provided many part-time jobs for me at home so that I could make some extra income without being away from home. As my daughter entered school, I moved into a part-time job as our first Preschool Director at my church. I am now working fulltime as a second grade teacher. I can tell you that during the past twenty years as a mother, Mark and I cannot tell you of one thing we ever needed and did not have. I know there were some things we wanted and couldn't afford, but I cannot remember what they were. What I do remember is the joy and happiness I experienced in being where God desired for me to be.

I am certain that God wants us to give up the 'issue' of working and obediently seek out the answers of our callings. The world would have us tell our children they can grow up to be anything 'they' want to be or do. When my daughter was very young, I began teaching her that she could be anything that God chooses for her. I want her to learn now that it is not her choice if she wants her life to be successful and significant.

In the previous chapter, I made reference to the two main reasons for a woman's rebellion toward her husband's authority. The first one is determined by your expectations for his spiritual condition. I will share the second one with you now. It has to do with your desire to do God's will in relation to your callings. God's will is for you to follow your calling of helpmeet while you live in submission to your husband. God will take care of the rest and you must trust Him in this matter. God never meant for your love toward Him to cause you feelings of conflict. If you love God, and desire to serve Him, He knows your heart. If your husband is standing in the way of God's call in your life, you must still continue in submission to him until God works out the details. He will do this when His timing is perfect. You do not have to choose between God and your husband so do not try. Do you remember that direct line you have with God? You don't have to move away from your place in the chain of command in order to serve God or have a relationship with Him. He knows your heart, but what he wants is your obedience. When you choose to live in submission to your husband, you are obeying God.

Write Philippians 1:6:

Who is going to complete the work God has begun in you through your callings?

Where do you believe you are getting in God's way right now in your life because of lack of trust in God's timing?

God can and will complete all that He has begun in your life but you must allow Him the opportunity. I pray that you do not miss out on something precious in your life because of your lack of trust. Take what you wrote above and complete the prayer below.

Dearest, most precious Lord, I do know that your timing is perfect and I pray that you will help me trust you as I wait patiently for _____

_____

in my life. I know that you love me and will complete ALL that YOU have begun in my life.

> "And (she) who loses (her) life
> (By finding her success and significance in me)
> For my sake shall find it.
> (And custom-designed callings)
> Matthew 10:39

Meeting His Needs Physically

Why?

Write 1 Corinthians 7:2-5:

First of all, we see in verse two, the issue of immorality. The Greek word for immorality is porneia. The KJV translation is fornication. It means idolatry, unlawful lust, or to commit immorality. The word fornication refers to the act of sex. The word lust refers to the desire for sex. The word idolatry is the worship of anything having to do with sex in a wrongful way, which means that committing sin in this area is more important than obedience to God. My pastor recently pointed out the similarity in the words pornography and porneia. One definition for the word pornography refers to the life and manners of prostitutes. Another definition refers to the expression or suggestion of obscene or unchaste subjects in literature and art. These two areas of pornography are everywhere. If there is a man who struggles with this temptation, he will not have to look far to be satisfied.

Your husband may not have a problem with pornography, but that doesn't mean he can't be tempted. Author and speaker, James Dobson, (7) once said that his wife, Shirley, asked him how she could pray for him in this area of sexual temptation. James Dobson travels a great deal, but he told Shirley that he knew he could not easily be tempted by a prostitute because he had once been approached by one on an elevator in a motel where he was staying. He told her, however, that if he were to be tempted, it would more likely be with someone he worked with on a regular basis. When men and women work closely together, there is always a tremendous opportunity for a close friendship to develop into a desire for more. Please don't assume this could never happen to you or to your husband. Pray for yourself and for him in this area. Remember Jeremiah 33:3? We have seen it a lot in this study. If there is a woman you need to be concerned about in your husband's life, pray that God will *beep* you on that built in beeper. He will do it! He has done it for me a few times. Then, you can pray for God to keep that relationship as it should be. Don't worry! Just let Him take care of it. The potential for immorality is the first very important reason for you to make certain you are providing your husband's needs physically. The Greek word for 'have' in verse two is scheo and is translated to hold, such as possession, nearness, and intimacy. You need to strive for these elements in your marriage.

A man's body was designed by God to need sexual activity on a regular basis. If you are not providing this for him, then he will have to provide it himself by unnatural means. If he is not allowing you to meet his needs, you should be on your knees, every day, praying that God will bring him to the point of repentance toward his unnatural means of meeting those physical needs.

The second issue we see in verse three is that of 'duty'! The KJV translation is render. The Greek word is iodide. It means to give away, to give up, to give over or back, deliver, give again, payment, perform, or yield. The word 'duty' means obligation and responsibility. You are obligated 'to' your husband in this area, and you are responsible 'for' your husband in this area. The KJV refers to marital duty as due benevolence. The Greek word for 'due' is opheilo, which means accruing, owe, to under obligation or debt. Most biblical translations refer to money; however, this translation is referring to marital debt or duty. The Greek word for benevolence is eunoia which means kindness, conjugal duty, or goodwill. It is from a root word, eunoeo, which means to be well minded, reconcile, or agree. In other words, please don't roll your eyes or make a face when your husband requires you physically.

Verse four refers to the wife's relinquishing of power over her own body. We have referred to this several times in our study. The Greek word for power is exousiazo, which means to control, exercise authority upon, or bring under the power of. As a wife, you are to let go of all these areas of power. You have no right to say no to your husband except by agreement, as verse five points out. Do not use sex as a means of revenge or getting back at your husband. Treat him as you would like to be treated in this area.

Verse five says 'do not deprive one another'. The Greek word here for deprive is postereo which is translated to despoil, defraud, kept back in fraud. The word defraud means to cheat, swindle, or trick. Have you ever lay in bed pretending to be asleep or lied about a headache? You are depriving your husband by fraud or trickery when you do this. Do you remember the key to meeting your husband's needs emotionally? It is submission! Do not try to cheat or trick your husband with flimsy excuses when he needs you physically. Submission in this area refers to willingness as we saw in the word 'benevolence'. Your husband should never feel as if you are only performing a 'duty'. He needs to feel kindness and good will in this area. God created you to meet that husband's needs and that includes his physical needs.

These verses also include his responsibility to you in this area.

Write 1 Peter 3:7:

Your husband is living in sin if he is not meeting your needs physically. Again, you need to pray hard for him in this area. I will remind you, however, of the importance of an unselfish prayer. Your primary goal for your husband should be his spiritual condition. When that is right, everything else will fall into place. Remember, do not undermine him by trying to preach to him about this subject. Gently remind him of your need and desire for him without nagging. If you go around feeling sorry for yourself, you will not be able to make his spiritual condition a primary goal in your life.

The final warning of our passage in 1 Corinthians is the importance of always coming back together to avoid Satan's temptation because of a lack of self-control. Temptation is a tremendous burden on a person. It means through, across, beyond, farther, other side, or over. Satan will not ever stop trying to tempt your husband across to the other side no matter who he is, or how strong he is spiritually. You have seen over and over again how to build a hedge of protection around your home and family. Meeting his needs physically is no exception. Your ability to be tempted is just as strong. Don't ever assume it could not happen to you.

Physical needs are important to your husband and he needs to feel as if they are important to you. The keys to meeting his needs physically are willingness and availability. You are to be willing to meet his needs whenever he expresses a desire. The dishes can wait. You can put a marker in that book you are reading. Losing a little sleep will not kill you and I have heard that sexual activity releases tension that causes many headaches. So, no more flimsy excuses! Be glad that you are able to provide this need. God created you perfectly for that purpose!

How?

The Song of Songs gives us some wonderful advice on meeting his needs physically. This book deals with several important aspects of lovemaking that I want to share with you.

First of all, there is the aspect of admiration. When was the last time you complimented your husband on his looks? Some of you are thinking, well he never compliments me! That is not the point. You have got to learn how to lose yourself in the area of physical needs, and be what you know he wants and needs. I believe men need to know that their wives enjoy the way they look.

In chapter 5, verses 10-12, the beloved admires her lover.

Read the following verses and write the adjectives she uses to describe her lover:

Example: radiant, ruddy
1:16
5:10-12

She is admiring his appearance in a beautiful way. I believe it would be difficult for any man not to be affected by his wife's admiration.

She also admires how he makes her feel when they are intimate.

Read 5: 13,16-17 and write the descriptive passages she uses:

In Song of Solomon, 2:16, the beloved says, "My lover is mine and I am his, he browses among the lilies." She is expressing her desire for him, but mostly her availability to him. The word browse is translated 'feedeth' in the KJV. The Hebrew word is ra<ah which means to graze, pasture, to rule, keep company, devour, or eat up. She is rendering herself to him, and she says he is doing the same for her. She is giving herself freely, and with pleasure and joy. If you are having difficulty finding the pleasure and joy, you need to begin praying that God will bring it your way. Your husband needs to feel this from you. You may even be pleasantly surprised at the joy that comes your way as you give of yourself with little or no thought for your own needs. I once heard Adrian Rogers say that joy is an inside job and happiness is an outside job. You can work on the joy in this area of your relationship and let God bring the happiness your way when He is ready.

What about him?

Finally, let us look at the way the lover responds throughout this book. The majority of what we hear from him has to do with his description of the way his beloved looks. In chapter 1, verse 15, he says, "How beautiful you are my darling! Oh, how beautiful!" At the beginning of chapter 4, he calls her beautiful again. In the next 14 verses, he describes the beauty of every part of her body. In verse 9, he expresses the desire and arousal that comes his way because of her physical beauty. In chapter 6, we hear from him again as he says, "You are beautiful…lovely as Jerusalem…" he goes on, once again, to describe the beauty of different areas of her body and their affect on him. Chapter 7 also begins with more admiration of particular body parts as he even admires her feet and calls them beautiful. There is little else that we hear from the lover. I think we can safely conclude from these passages that the man is very aroused by the woman's appearance.

On my wedding day, I asked my dad for advice. He looked at me with that mischievous grin, and said, "Don't go to bed with curlers in your hair." He was trying to be his usual witty self, but I also heard the wisdom in his words. He was telling me the importance of my appearance around my husband, especially at times of intimacy. I have always tried very hard to heed his precious words.

I do believe, however, that our inner beauty is a very important element in our ability to be more attractive to our husbands. I truly believe that if he can love you from the inside, you will be even more beautiful on the outside. The lover made reference to his beloved's inner beauty in Song of Solomon 6:9.

Write 1 Peter 3: 3-5

Your ability to meet your husband's needs physically is also reflected in the way you dress and act around other men. Inner beauty is truly going to be seen in this area. We have seen how easily the man is aroused by the woman's body. So why do we tend to go around showing so much to other men, when it is meant to be exclusive for our husbands?

I have always been curious as to how 1 Corinthians 11: 5 could apply to us as women today.

Read 1 Corinthians 11: 5 now:

Paul's advice is considered to be too conservative and untimely by many women. I believe, however, that Paul's wisdom was tremendous, because he was very aware of the chemistry between men and women. Paul was advising the Corinthians on public worship in chapter 11. A woman with an uncovered head was considered to be reflecting loose morals or sexual promiscuity. His advice is concerned with the actions of men and women showing only glory to God in public worship, rather than bringing attention to them.

What Paul is referring to in 11:5 is not a degrading reflection on the woman, but rather a strong understanding of the woman's ability to distract a man. When a woman comes to church dressed inappropriately, it is highly possible that she will keep a man from worshipping as God intended. My mother raised me to dress appropriately (modestly) around men, especially in church. If a woman is going to a public worship service for the right reasons, she should dress appropriately as not to be an obstacle in a man's ability to worship. Let your husband be the one to see those beautiful body parts, not everyone else's husband. In Song of Solomon, 7:1, the lover refers to his beloved's feet and legs. He is very aware of every part of her body and how it all works together in his natural instinct to be aroused. When a woman comes to church showing cleavage or most of her legs, who is it that she is trying to glorify with her dress? My first response would be herself.

Write Romans 14:13:

Allow your husband to see the purity you reflect in this area. Save yourself for him exclusively. The lover and the beloved make reference to belonging to each other exclusively in Song of Songs. Does your husband feel that you are his exclusively and in every way? I certainly hope that mine does!

So while you are exclusively expressing your willingness and availability to him, you can also try to be as attractive as possible, inside and out. Talk to him if you need or just listen to what he might be saying. After all, wouldn't you rather have him look your way, or remember how you looked, smelled, or felt as he left you for the day? Pray as he leaves you each day, that you will be foremost on his mind. Also, begin admiring, desiring, and enjoying as you willingly make yourself available to him. Your husband will love it!

> "Not only must the inner sanctuary be kept right with God, but
> the outer courts as well are to be brought into perfect accord with
> the purity God gives us by His grace." (8)
> Oswald Chambers

My Utmost for His Highest

Part Four

Meeting His Needs Spiritually

16

$\mathcal{E}$xtreme $\mathcal{S}$easons

Strength and honor are her clothing;
And she shall rejoice in time to come.
Proverbs 31:25

The NIV translation says:

She is clothed with strength and dignity;
She can laugh at the days to come.

Leah's mother had come to take Abigail and Levi home with her, and Leah had enjoyed a quiet day at home. She thought of Psalm 140:4 as she pondered her last few visits with Sarah. "Keep me, O Lord, from the hands of the wicked; preserve me from violent men, who have purposed to make my steps stumble." Sarah had not admitted any abuse from Jacob but Leah was certain that her bruises were a result of Jacob's unexplained anger. Leah decided this was the perfect day to visit Sarah and try to bring her some cheer.

When Leah arrived at Sarah's home, a neighbor greeted her with news that Sarah was very ill and staying with her parents. Leah rushed to Sarah's side and found her unresponsive to anyone. "She will not tell us anything," said Sarah's mother. "We know that Jacob is hurting her but she would not leave him. Her father found her like this and carried her here. Leah, she will not even look our way when we speak to her. Maybe she will respond to you. Leah, please try!" she pleaded.

Leah sat beside the bed as she ran her fingers through Sarah's beautiful, thick brown hair. "Talk to me, Sarah," said Leah softly. "I'm the only one here. What is going on?" "I am a terrible wife, Leah," said

Sarah. "I can't do anything right. I can't make Jacob happy no matter how hard I try. Leah, right now, I just want to die!" Leah fought back the tears as she continued to run her fingers through Sarah's hair. "Leah," said Sarah, "I know that Jacob is not a believer and I remember the apostle Paul saying that the believing wife should not leave her unbelieving husband."

"Sarah," said Leah, "Paul suggested that you should not divorce your unbelieving husband, but for now, you need to stay with your parents until you are better. They already know he is hurting you and they can pray with you and help hold Jacob accountable for his actions." "I love Jacob, Leah, and I want him to believe," said Sarah, "but he doesn't listen. Leah, Benjamin changed greatly after you married. He must love you so much! Please tell me how you managed such a change in your husband."

Leah laughed quietly. "Sarah, it was God that changed Benjamin. Not me! My time with Lydia taught me how to be a door between Benjamin and God. Sarah, I would have made Benjamin miserable if I had not followed God's design for marriage." Sarah carefully sat up in the bed and Leah saw a glimmer in her eyes. "Leah, will you please teach me what you did?" "I so want Jacob to be like Benjamin!" "Sarah," Leah laughed, "You will make Jacob miserable if you expect him to be like Benjamin." "You must never expect him to be like any other person other than who God made him to be. So goes your first lesson, Sarah," said Leah. "You rest and we will talk more when you are better. Just promise me you will stay here until you know God is ready for you to return." "I will, said Sarah. "I will!"

Extreme Seasons

This woman is clothed with strength and honor. These qualities are precious and they are a direct result of her ability to rejoice or laugh at the days to come. They also provide her with the ability to laugh at the days to come. The word *rejoice* is translated to laugh in pleasure or detraction. When I began studying this verse, I first looked at how this translation was used elsewhere in the Old Testament. I will share some of this with you later in the chapter, but first I would like for us to study the word 'laugh'.

The translation for 'laugh' referred to laughing in pleasure or detraction. I discovered the word 'detraction' means 'insult'. Let me share some synonyms for 'insult' with you now. First, there is the word 'affront' which means to insult to the face or make to feel ashamed. It also means 'not to honor'. Another synonym for detraction is the word 'aspersion'. This word refers to slander or false charges made against a person. Then, we come to the word 'abuse'. One meaning for 'abuse' is neglect or abandonment. It even refers to discarding. It also means mistreatment, corruption, and perversion. Another meaning for abuse refers to violation which means breach or rape. 'Breach' refers to the action of breaking. Abuse also refers to the action of maligning with words. Today, we would call this 'verbal abuse'. We keep going as we find another synonym in the word 'censure'. This word means condemnation through judgment. It also refers to hostile criticism, unfavorable opinion, blaming and finding fault.

Are you beginning to see, as I did, that this woman had learned to laugh in some extreme seasons and situations? This is not your everyday adversity. Many of you reading this chapter have some form of 'detraction' or 'insult' in your life. Many of you have faced this from someone you love or loved, maybe even your husband. This detraction could be anything from neglect to verbal abuse or even physical abuse.

Proverbs 31:25 gives some very wise and timely advice for ways to handle this abuse. First of all, laugh at the days to come. Some of you are already thinking that laughing is the last thing you would do in any of these situations. This 'laughing' actually refers more to an understanding that God is in control and there is eternal victory no matter what happens. Remember, she was clothed in strength and honor. This translation for strength refers to force, security, boldness, might, and power. It is taken from a root word meaning harden or prevail. We have seen all of these qualities in her throughout this study. She knows she will prevail in the end because all of these virtues are from the Lord. She understands that she is in no way responsible for her abuse. She is not to blame and her strength is the strength of the Lord.

The word 'honor' is translated magnificence, ornament, splendor, beauty, and excellency. She carries her godliness and godly virtues in ways that show through to everyone, even that person who is abusing her.

So, what about that physical abuse? What if that husband has put your life or the life of your children in danger with his physical violence? One translation for 'laugh' refers to laughing with scorn. The word scorn means to shun. Shun means to seek safety by concealment or flight from an enemy or his pursuit. It means to evade a blow or to avoid from fear or caution; to keep away from, to escape, to shrink back physically, to move or go away. The word shun is an abbreviation of the word attention. This was new to me and I found it to be very interesting. The word shun does not refer to completely cutting yourself off from a person, but rather getting their attention by removing yourself from the violence.

At the beginning of this chapter, I told you that I had studied other uses of this translation. In the Psalms, David referred several times to the Lord's laughter at those who sought to destroy him.

Write Psalm 37:13:

Write Ezekiel 33:11:

Is God glad the wicked will perish?

Why is God laughing?

He is laughing because He knows the righteous will be vindicated through His judgment of the wicked. He laughs because He knows His power will one day provide the victory

Psalm 59:8 says, "But you, O Lord, laugh at them; you scoff at all those nations." To 'scoff' means that He holds extreme contempt for their behavior. A woman can laugh at the extreme situations in her life because she knows her Lord is in heaven laughing with her. He knows the future of her enemies. He holds their behavior in extreme contempt. He will be victorious in his dealings with them.

Paul had learned this lesson well. He wrote in 2 Corinthians 12:10, "Therefore I am well content with weaknesses, with insults, with distresses, with persecutions, with difficulties for Christ's sake; for when I am weak, then I am strong." (NAS) The Greek word for insults is translated a reproaches in the KJV. It is very similar to the Hebrew translation for detraction. It refers to insolence (as in overbearing), harm, injury, and hurt. It is from a root word which means to place you above or over another. Paul had faced insult and abuse in his life. Paul was clothed with strength, had lost himself 'for Christ's sake', and had found himself on the other side of his abuse. God can and will give you the same strength to face your times of detraction.

A woman in this situation must continue to live a godly life, allowing God to show her how to handle her situation. In times like these, you must remember that you are the only one with your direct line to Christ. He will tell you what to do. He may tell you to stay or he may tell you to remove yourself for a time. If you listen to the voices of others, you will become frustrated and confused. Pray that God will reveal to you the godly counsel of others and especially show you when to disregard ungodly counsel.

Write Psalm 1:1:

We have seen Jesus as our example over and over again throughout our study. Those who loved Him wanted to spare His pain and His life on the cross. In Matthew 26:42, even Jesus prayed, "… my Father, if it is possible for this cup to be taken away unless I drink it, may your will be done." (NIV) Jesus knew the abuse He would face. He asked his Father whether he might possibly be removed from the abuse. The cross He bore was necessary for our salvation. 1 Corinthians 7:16-17 says, "For what knowest thou, O wife, whether thou shalt save thy husband…? But as God hath distributed to every man, as the Lord hath called everyone, so let him walk." (KJV) The word 'called' is translated 'to bid', and is a commandment. The word walk is to live, follow, or be occupied. Jesus wanted God's will in His life above all else. God will direct you to the path He desires for you to take and He will be with you as you travel that path. He will go before you or carry you as your needs require.

Do you believe God is powerful enough to protect you if you follow His will and clothe you with strength and honor?

In 1 Samuel 25, there is a story about a woman named Abigail. Her husband's name was Nabal. Nabal is described as being churlish and evil. The word churlish is translated as severe, cruel, grievous, hard, rough, stiff-necked, stubborn, and in trouble. Another translation is impudent which means insolent. The word insolent means insulting. Does that sound familiar? Some synonyms for 'churlish' are contemptuous, disrespectful, impertinent, overbearing, rude, and bold. One last translation is obstinate which means stubborn, uncontrollable, callous, and prejudiced. Some synonyms for this word are mulish, headstrong, deaf, firm, dogged and bullheaded. Are you getting a nice, clear picture of Nabal? Well, we have only begun drawing this picture. The word evil means bad, grievous, harmful, hurtful, mischievous, naughty, wicked, wretched, and wrong. It is taken from a root word which means to spoil by breaking into little pieces, to make good for nothing physically, socially, and morally. It means to afflict, breakdown in pieces, and even to show self friendly to someone by mistake in order to use them. I think we can safely assume that Abigail lived in an extreme situation with Nabal.

In chapter 25 of 1 Samuel, Nabal refuses to help David by not providing supplies even though David had watched over his property and his men. Abigail went to him and pleaded for him not to harm her household. She was willing to take responsibility for her husband's actions in order to protect her family and household. I believe Abigail knew full well how Nabal would react when she told him of her meeting with David. I believe the chances are great that Abigail would have experienced physical violence from Nabal. I also believe we can strongly assume she had been abused in the past. God was finished with this violent, stiff-necked man. God was in heaven laughing at the futile wickedness of Nabal. The bottom line here is that God loves you more than you can ever know or understand. How much do you love him? How much are you willing to endure to bring that husband into his presence? God desires a relationship with that unsaved, disobedient husband. He knows whether your husband's heart is hardened or whether he is reachable through your behavior. Can you laugh at the future along with God because you know He is waiting there for you? Do you believe that He is waiting there with His love, protection, and victory for your life?

We find God's protection for Abigail in 1 Samuel 25:37 when she "...told him all these things, and his heart failed him and he became like stone. About ten days later the Lord struck Nabal and he died." God would not allow Abigail to be hurt again. He was there with love, protection, and victory for her life. Now, don't get me wrong. God's protection over you will most likely not involve killing off your husband, but He will protect you if you obediently follow the path He has provided for you.

There is a beautiful passage in Ecclesiastes, chapter 3 that refers to a time for everything. Verse one says, "There is a time for everything and a season for everything under heaven." (NIV) Verse four says, "A time to weep and a time to laugh..." The translation for laugh is the same translations in proverbs 31:25 for rejoice. The translation for season in Ecclesiastes 3:1 is similar to the translation for night in Proverbs 31. It refers to an appointed occasion or time. Every season is appointed by God and under

His control. If we are living in His will and obediently following His calling in our life, we need only find peace in every circumstance that fills our seasons, even those extreme ones.

Stress is a direct result of our inability to handle our circumstances. Satan wants us to be stressed because he knows we are relying on ourselves and not God. When we know we are living within God's will, there is no reason to assume our circumstances point to our downfall. Laugh at those circumstances today and tomorrow as this woman did. They serve to grow us and I have come to appreciate my growth experiences.

The words 'time to come' in Proverbs 31:25 refer to her ability to be at peace about the future. She is not worried or anxious because she is confident about what God is doing in the life of her family. (See Philippians 4:10-13) Jesus taught his disciples the importance of a peaceful heart without worry of the future.

Write Matthew 6:34

I don't want to leave you with an entirely negative feeling about Proverbs 31:25 because the translation referred to her ability to laugh in times of pleasure as well. It also referred to laughing as in sport. The word pleasure means enjoyment, delight, gladness, and gratification. The word 'sport' means playfulness, fun, amusement, recreation, or entertainment. This woman knew how to have fun and how to play and laugh with her family. Taking time to have fun with your family is so important. I have recently joined Facebook and one of my favorite things to do is read the statuses of young mothers, especially when they are talking about the things they do with their families.

I also think it is crucial for you, as a woman, to take some time doing things that please you. Two other meanings for pleasure are indulgence and preference. Preference refers to doing things that reflect your own taste, fondness, or partiality. Indulgence means gratification and excess. In other words, take the time to indulge yourself with the things that bring you pleasure. Indulgence also refers to tolerance. This means open-mindedness. Have fun with your family by being open-minded about the things they like to do. I once rode a roller coaster with my daughter, and went on a four mile cave tour with my husband. Both required a tremendous amount of open-mindedness on my part, but I had fun and laughed a lot because I knew I was bringing pleasure into their lives.

This brave woman has learned to laugh with God. She also has learned to laugh with her family. She indulges them and herself. She is confident. Her confidence, however, is not in herself, but in her Lord who has allowed her to find herself in Him.

> "…and (she) that loseth (her) life
> (During her extreme seasons)
> For my sake shall find it."
> (And a time of rejoicing in every season)
> Matthew 10:30

17

$\mathcal{C}$onfident $\mathcal{C}$ommunication

"She openeth her mouth with wisdom,
And in her tongue is the law of kindness."
Proverbs 31:26

Leah and Sarah sat at the small table in the home of Sarah's parents. It had been three weeks since Leah had seen Sarah and she was pleased at how much better she was, both physically and emotionally. "Jacob comes by every day," said Sarah. "Leah, yesterday he wept as he begged me to go home with him. If only I thought I could trust him," said Sarah. "I want to be with him, but I know that I can't allow him to continue hurting me, Leah!"

"Sarah, you must continue to pray for Jacob. It is important that you know if there is an attempt on his part to learn how to manage his anger. Sarah, until Jesus Christ becomes Lord of his life, you know you risk being hurt when he becomes angry, but you have to understand that you are not responsible for his anger. Jacob is angry with himself, not with you. That is what Paul meant when he said "...For how do you know, O (believing) wife, whether you will save your husband...". (1 Corinthians 7:16) If you choose to stay with him, there is a chance you can have a positive influence on his life that will allow him to come to know Christ as he sees Him represented in your life. Sarah, there is no guarantee this will happen so you have to decide whether you are willing to take this risk. If you choose to stay, I will teach you what I know and help you as much as I can, but you ultimately must depend on God to give you the strength you will need each and every day."

"Leah, I just don't know if I love Jacob enough to stay with him, but I do know how much I love God! I know that if I leave Jacob, I am choosing myself and my own happiness. If I stay with Jacob, I am choosing God and trusting his protection over me. I know in my heart that I want to be where God would desire for me to be. I also know that Jesus died on that cross for Jacob and that God placed me in his life. Leah, I know in my heart that I have to try and be a door for Jacob. I have to try and help him find God!"

Confident Communication

I love the word study with this verse as I discovered the translations refer to a woman's desire to disciple, exhort, and counsel others concerning the biblical precepts she has come to know and depend on. In chapter sixteen, we saw the confidence she has gained. This confidence fills her with the boldness needed to share with others. This woman opens her mouth with wisdom because she has been on the mountain top with God as well as through a great many valleys. She has developed a relationship with God that has helped her discover who He is. She has found herself in him. Now she is ready to share her God with others. One translation for the word kindness is beauty. The word kindness is taken from a root word which means to bow the neck in courtesy to an equal, to be kind, show self merciful, and put to shame. She has learned to communicate her God through her teaching and her behavior.

Are you beginning to see the domino effect in this passage? It will not fall into place unless we start at the beginning, putting each piece in its respective place! Leave out a piece and the chain reaction comes to an end. Put each piece into place and there is no stopping the picture that will form before your very eyes. I believe his woman takes every opportunity to instruct her children and her friends. The teachings of God are on her tongue just waiting for another opportunity to be shared.

We have already seen the importance of our need to steer away from any undermining of our husbands spiritual conditions. I'll never forget the day, many years ago, when my husband told me I was self-righteous. It broke my heart, but he was right! I had been preaching to him again, and it was the last time! We are now able to share spiritually with each other as we recognize the individual wisdom God has brought our way. I often call on Mark's wisdom and knowledge, but before we came to this point, I had to learn how to communicate mentally, emotionally, and spiritually with him.

One of the key factors in meeting the needs of our family members centers on communication. We have already seen the power that is possible in our submissive behavior and there is just as much power in our submissive communication. We have to learn how to 'teach' and not 'preach' to our husbands and children. There is a huge difference. The word *teach* means to instruct, inform, and inspire. I like that!

We are given a beautiful formula in scripture for communicating with others.

Write Ephesians 4:29:

What should NEVER come out of our mouths?

What should ALWAYS come out of our mouths?

This formula for communication should be used with our husbands, children, friends, co-workers, or anyone we might find ourselves communicating with. Whatever we say to our husbands should serve to encourage, build-up, and support them. Your speech should never attack, accuse, or attempt to control.

List some ways you tend to attack, accuse, or attempt to control your husband with your speech:

Write Proverbs 21:9

Write Proverbs 21:19

Go back and circle the places where it would be better for your husband to be than living with a wife that tries to control him with her speech!

The word 'contentious' is translated as quarrelsome or to cause strife. Is your speech making your husband miserable? This type of communication is not submissive.

Read Matthew 19:5:

What does this verse say a man should do to his wife?

Why?

My favorite translation for the word 'cleave' is to 'stick'. Your husband is commanded to 'stick' to you so that you can become one. I am convinced that many men are not able to do this because their wives will not allow them to 'stick'. Wives, we are like the two sides of Velcro. If you turn one piece the wrong way, the other side cannot stick. Which way are you turning today?

Many women push their husbands aside with threats. The woman who threatens her husband has not allowed the cleaving to take place. When you allow your husband to cleave unto you, what you are saying is, "I am here to stay, I am going nowhere, and I take my vows seriously!" I believe any woman who is not allowing her husband to 'stick' or 'cleave' should be living in fear of the Lord. The woman who is not cleaving to her husband has slammed 'shut' that door between him and God. She is saying I will open the door when I feel like it or when I feel like you deserve it. We do not 'cleave' when we feel like it! We adhere for all times, good, and bad. Becoming one makes you stronger as you learn to agree and work together.

Communication is a powerful thing.

When was the last time you tried to build your husband up according to his needs and not because you wanted something from him?

Are you trying to get your way or help him find his? Are you trying to talk your children into your expectations or help them find their way as they discover God's purpose in their lives?

> "…and (she) that loseth (her) life
> (With confident, supportive communication)
> For my sake shall find it."
> Matthew 10:39

18

$\mathcal{B}$uilt in '$\mathcal{B}$eepers'

"She looketh well to the ways of her household,
And eateth not the bread of idleness.
Proverbs 31:27

"**M**other, I will be glad to go harvest flax for you today," said Abigail. "Baby Luke is old enough to walk with us," said Leah. "We will go with you today." "Mother," said Abigail, "Stay home with Luke and I will take care of the flax." Leah felt something was going on with Abigail during the past few weeks. She had changed. She rarely talked to Leah and always seemed anxious to leave the house. Just that morning, Leah had prayed Jeremiah 32:40-41 for Abigail.

Lord, inspire her to fear you so that she will never turn away from
You and surely plant her in the land that you have for her
With all your heart and soul.

"Let's all go together today," said Leah. "I need to get out of the house!"

Abigail shrugged her shoulders and said nothing. As they all walked toward the fields, Leah stopped to tend to Luke. Abigail kept walking and as she neared the fields, Leah noticed a young man running towards her. Leah watched as they spoke, then the man turned to look at her and ran off again. "Abigail, who was the young man?" asked Leah. "Just someone asking about work," said Abigail. Leah watched Abigail all morning and observed her to be very quiet and distant. She also noticed that Abigail was constantly looking back to the fields across from them where several men and women were harvesting flax. After several hours had passed, Leah decided to take Luke home. "Abigail," said Leah, "See if you can hire someone to help you carry the flax.

I will pay them when you arrive home." Leah saw a faint smile on Abigail's face as she looked across at the other fields. "Oh, yes, Mother," said Abigail, "I am sure I can find someone to help."

Later that day, Abigail arrived home and Leah recognized the young man with her. He was the man she had spoken with on their journey to the fields that morning. "I don't think we have met," said Leah. "I saw you talking with Abigail this morning." The young man's face turned red as he introduced himself. "My name is James," said the young man. "I journey and travel from city to city in order to preach and proclaim the good news of Jesus Christ." It just so happens that when you saw me this morning, I was asking Abigail if she knew of anyone who might hire me. I always try to find work when I am planning to stay awhile in a city." "Well, we might be able to use you around here for a few things, James. Please, come back and join us for supper. My husband, Benjamin, will tell you what is needed." James smiled at Abigail as he turned and walked away.

"Mother, don't you think he is so handsome?" said Abigail excitedly. "I have seen him almost every day for three weeks now. He always stops to greet me and he is so polite. Today is the first time he has stopped to talk and he really did ask me where to find work. I immediately went to find him after you left the fields." "He is a stranger, Abigail," said Leah. "You should never be alone with him, and your father will find out more tonight at supper."

After James had left that evening, Benjamin took Leah out of the house for a walk. "James is a very mature and wise young man," said Benjamin. "He asked when Abigail would be of betrothal age. He wants her to become his wife. He told me that he has asked many people in the city about her and they all have said she is a godly young woman and that all of the fathers are hoping their sons can become betrothed to her. He wanted me to know his intentions before anyone else has the opportunity to choose her. I have hired him to help with a few things but he knows he cannot be alone with her at any time or he will immediately lose his job." Leah felt such strange sensations in her stomach but she also felt a peace because she trusted Benjamin's instincts. She knew they could not tell Abigail any of this. In just two months, she would become of age for betrothal and James would come back to Benjamin for approval. By that time, they would know just what kind of man he is.

Built In 'Beepers'

I am especially fond of the message in this verse. For years I have prayed and searched for ways to protect my family. This verse is your key to tremendous hope for allowing God's protection in your home. God is the security system for your family. But you are the only one who can turn it on. Consider this verse and this chapter as your owner's manual.

The words 'looketh' and 'ways' are translated to show that she observes or watches their steps. "… eateth not the bread of idleness," refers to her continual efforts at this process of observation. We have some dear friends, who several years ago discovered their son was involved in drug use. His parents are godly people and his mother continually observed and watched the ways of their teenagers. Her determination to always know what was going on led her to realize something was wrong with her oldest son. There wasn't anything specific she could put her finger on, just mother's intuition. Her husband accused her of being paranoid until the day she found proof in her son's room. He got the help he needed and is now on track.

What if this mother had just assumed her son would never do anything like this? What if she had been too busy with her own affairs to realize that a problem existed? Never assume you have perfect children. Never assume there are certain things they would never do.

Write Romans 3:23

As sinners, our children struggle with the temptations of this world each and every day. It is our responsibility to observe their steps so that we can be there to help them through their struggles. They will always need our love and guidance.

Another dear friend began to realize her marriage was lacking something. Her husband seemed different. She began praying and watching. One night, she heard her husband up moving around. She heard him leave, which was not unusual in his line of work. This time, something made her get up out of bed. She picked up the phone, pressed the redial button, and heard the voice of another woman. She later confirmed that he was indeed involved with this woman. She was shocked as this was not something she thought her husband would do. She had begun to watch the ways of her household but as we spent time together, she confessed she had not been the wife she knew her husband needed. He wanted to try and hold the marriage together, so they moved to another city, away from the other woman. They are currently doing well and working hard at their marriage.

Our husbands and children are Satan's prey. We must have our 'beepers' on constantly in order to observe their steps because Satan does not rest! We can't either! We do, however, have hope. This godly design He has for us is our best hope for averting an unnecessary tragedy in our homes. Remember Jeremiah 33:3? All you have to do is ask and "He…will show you great and mighty things you do not know." Trust God to be your eyes and ears as he sharpens your keen senses. God has given you a built in 'beeper' to go along with that radar you have. If there is something you need to know, God will show you, but He cannot 'beep' you unless you are observing their steps continually. What you cannot see, God can see. You cannot watch over your family, however, if you are out searching for your own success and significance, away from God's will for your life. When you are not in God's will for your life, you are out of range from your 'beeper' signal. You will not hear it!

This is yet another wonderful way for you to protect that precious family. Watch and observe their steps continually, carefully, but lovingly. Don't assume, accuse, or attack without proof. Wait patiently for God to show you that proof when needed!

Keep laughing and having fun with your family and avoid the worry that will lead you to stress unnecessarily. You can be on call without watching your beeper every second. Keep your senses working, and God will beep you if there is an emergency!

> "And (she) that loseth (her) life
> (By continually observing the steps of her family)
> For my sake shall find it."
> (And more protection for her family!)

Stay in 'beeper' range!!!!

19

Loving Legacies

"Her children arise up and call her blessed;
Her husband also, and he praiseth her."
Proverbs 31:28

Leah wiped the tears from her eyes as she watched Abigail and James come out from their new home. It was time for the celebration of marriage to begin. Leah stood back and watched as family and friends congratulated the young couple. Abigail was beautiful and James looked so handsome and happy. He adored Abigail. Leah and Benjamin had been very impressed with James as they came to know him. They could not have found a more perfect husband for their daughter. He loved Abigail, but he loved God even more. Leah knew she would miss the girl talks she had enjoyed for years with Abigail. She would miss Abigail's helpful spirit around the house, and she was so good with Levi and Luke. Leah knew her daughter would be a wonderful mother. She thought about the times they had talked about marriage during her betrothal year of waiting for James to come for her. Leah prayed she had taught her everything she needed to know.

In the midst of her thoughts, she looked up to see Abigail standing in front of her. "Mother," said Abigail, "Don't be sad." "God has used you and father to prepare me for this marriage. I am ready." "James and I want to make God the center of our marriage just like you and father did."

Benjamin walked over to them and wrapped his arms around Leah and Abigail. "Abigail," he said, "The proudest and happiest day of my life was the day I married your mother." "I know she has taught you many things to prepare you for marriage, but you will still need to depend on God every single day." "Your mother taught me how important it is to depend on Him and have a personal relationship with Him. Abigail, James already has that relationship and he is exactly the kind of man your mother and I have prayed would become your husband."

Abigail wiped a few tears from her eyes as she hugged her parents. "God's blessings abound in our family," said Abigail, "And, Mother, you are blessed among women! I love you very much!

The word blessed is translated to be straight, especially to be level, right, and happy, to go forward, be honest, and prosper. Her children recognize all that she is and all that she has as a unique woman. The verse says her husband also calls her blessed. Not only that, but he praiseth her. Remember what we learned in our lesson on meekness? "Blessed are the meek, for they will inherit the earth." (Matthew 5:5) The virtuous woman is claiming her inheritance and passing it along to her children and husband.

The word 'praiseth' is translated to be clear as in his verbal praise. It also means to make a show, to boast, to rave, celebrate, or to shine. Her husband is almost embarrassing in his praise for his wife.

There is a woman in the Song of Solomon who was blessed and praised in the same way by those who knew her.

Read Solomon 6:9

This woman was the 'choice' one. The Hebrew translation for choice in this verse is to be beloved, pure, clean, and empty. She has emptied herself. Wow! Are you seeing this picture? This woman has emptied herself only to become filled with Jesus Christ. She has lost herself and those who know her praise her virtuous qualities. The NIV translation for choice is unique. She is 'uniquely' woman. She has learned to follow God's design for her life, the only design that will result in these qualities.

Name some things that keep you from following this design for becoming 'uniquely woman' and tell why:

Example-pride because my human nature causes me to feel I should have something to offer

The woman in proverbs 31:28 has discovered the ultimate reward or blessing that comes from being 'uniquely' woman is to be 'uniquely loved'! Isn't that the most exciting prospect, to be loved and praised by your family in the most perfect way? How wonderful to have a precious, unique love that can only come if you strive to become uniquely woman. The legacy of being uniquely woman is the unique love of her family, a family that has inherited her love for God!

This woman has given up her quest for success and significance, and found it. She has also given up the quest for happiness, but yet, her life is full of happiness and joy. Did you even notice that one of the translations for blessed is happiness? When the virtuous woman stopped pursuing happiness, and settled into joy, she found it! Another translation is 'prosper'. When she gave up her quest for success and significance, and settled into sacrifice, she found it! She has given up her life for the sake of her Lord, and she has found it. She enjoys a happy lifestyle and circumstances because she has learned to accept, appreciate, and laugh at them. Her joy is contagious! It has poured over her family and they are reaping the rewards. Her family serves to strengthen her with their praise and love. The verse says her children and her husband 'arise' in proverbs 31:28 and this is translated to strengthen, accomplish, confirm, continue, decree, make good, help, hold, lift up, establish, and remain. Can you imagine your family doing all of this for you? I realize the picture may be difficult to imagine, but it is possible. She started out 'arising' for them, and now they are returning the love!

I am thinking of several precious women in our church whose children 'arise' up and bless their mothers in this way. I also see how their husband's hearts trust in them with love and praise. What a legacy!

It is time to stop and carefully consider your own life again. What kind of legacy are you creating?

From where is your success and significance coming?

In her book, The Desires of a Woman's Heart, (9) Beverly LaHaye says, "Happiness is not a goal to be sought, but a byproduct of a life in obedience to God." She also says, "What is the root of happiness? Knowing and obeying God. God wants each of his children to be happy."

You may have a wonderful husband, beautiful children, a well paying, successful job, but, do you fall into bed at night with a smile on your face because you really feel successful? Do you truly feel that you have it all, or does all of 'it' have you? How much time do you spend striving for things that will remain behind when you leave this world? The blessings and happiness that come from being uniquely woman are far reaching. They will go to heaven with you. Amen!

> "…And (she) that loseth (her) life
> For my sake shall find it."
> (And a legacy of love)

20

Eternal Security

> Many daughters have done virtuously,
> But thou excellest them all. Favor is deceitful,
> And beauty is vain; but a woman that feareth the lord,
> She shall be praised. Give her the fruit of her hands;
> And let her own works praise her in the gates."
> Proverbs 31:29-31

Benjamin sat in the dark room with his head in his hands. *How could she be gone? Leah had been the greatest blessing of his life and now she was gone. How could he go on without her?* A soft knock at the door stirred his grief as he called, "Enter." Benjamin looked up. He saw all of his children, their spouses, and his eight precious grandchildren standing in the room. "Oh, how your grandmother, Leah, loved you!" he said as he looked at each child.

Abigail was amazed as she looked around the small house and saw more food than any of them would be able to eat. "Everyone loved her," she said softly. "None more that I!" replied Benjamin.

"She is being praised at the Heavenly Gates today, Father!" exclaimed Abigail. "Her frail hands are working once again for Jesus." Benjamin smiled at Abigail's sentiments. "She was miserable these last few years," he said sadly. "She would sit and stare at her spinning wheel with tears in her eyes. She always wanted to use her hands to help others, but the years of spinning and weaving took their toll on her beautiful hands."

"Mother is spinning in heaven right now as she sings her beautiful songs to Jesus! I can almost hear her singing, Father!" "Abigail," said Benjamin, "I cannot tell you how many times I have awakened from my sleep because I thought I heard her singing." Benjamin began sobbing as Levi walked over to hold his father. "We will all be together again someday," said Levi softly as he wiped tears from his own eyes. "Levi," said Benjamin, "Your mother's greatest joy was knowing that all of her children and grandchildren had accepted Christ as their personal savior. She prayed for each of you every day by name."

Levi began laughing as he shared about the time he had awakened to find his mother praying over him. "I screamed and woke everyone up because I didn't know it was mother." They all laughed and began sharing their stories and memories of their precious Leah. Benjamin picked up the small pillow with the embroidered bird Leah had made for him. As the stories slowly began to fade, Abigail softly began to sing from Psalm 112,

> *"Blessed is the (woman) who fears the Lord,*
> *Who finds great delight in His commands,*
> *(Her) children will be mighty in the land;*
> *The generation of the upright will be blessed.*
> *Wealth and riches are in her house,*
> *And (her) righteousness endures forever.*
> *Even in darkness, light dawns for the upright*
> *For the gracious, compassionate and upright (woman).*
> *Good will come to (her) who is generous and lends freely,*
> *Who conducts her affairs with justice.*
> *Surely (she) will never be shaken;*
> *A righteous (woman) will be forever remembered,*
> *(She) will have no fear of bad news;*
> *(Her) heart is steadfast, trusting in the Lord,*
> *(Her) heart is secure; (she) will have no fear;*
> *In the end (she) will look in triumph on (her) foes.*
> *(She) has scattered abroad (her) gifts to the poor.*
> *(Her) righteousness endures forever.*
> *(Her) horn will be lifted high in honor…"*

Eternal Security

These verses are what I call a living eulogy. It sums up the passage of a dead woman, a woman who is dead to herself and alive in Jesus Christ. Her rewards are great. She has received them all. Everything she has done and is doing is known and talked about at the gates. Remember the gates?

Elisabeth Elliot (10) once said, "How do we expect to follow one who took up a cross and not encounter suffering? When the will of God cuts across the will of man, somebody has to die. Leaders are meant to be losers of ourselves and of our rights."

We lost our rights at the Garden of Eden. We found them again at the foot of the cross. Why is it so difficult for us to make our home right there in His presence? He wants us there! He waits for us there! It is where I long to be!

This passage in Proverbs paints the process of death for this Godly woman. She learns how to die to herself in service to God and others through sacrifice. It doesn't happen overnight. It is a lifelong process that happens through the seasons of her life. In her death experience she finds who she is and was created to be, and she finds peace in this purpose.

The final reward for the Godly woman is eternal life with her Father in Heaven, where she will be praised at heaven's Gates! AMEN!

> "…And (she) that loseth (her) life
> For my sake shall find it." Matthew 10:39
> (And eternal life with her heavenly father)

Meeting His Needs Spiritually

Why?

"Davidd, wearing a linen ephod, danced before the Lord with all his might, while he and the entire house of Israel brought up the Ark of the Lord with shouts and the sound of trumpets. As the Ark of the Lord was entering the city of David, Michal, daughter of Saul, watched from the window. And when she saw King David (her husband) leaping and dancing before the Lord, she despised him in her heart." 2 Samuel 6: 14-16

"When David returned home to bless his household, Michal, daughter of Saul, came out to meet him and said, "How the King of Israel distinguished himself today, disrobing in the sight of the slave girls of his servants as any vulgar fellow would." David said to Michal, "It was before the Lord, who chose me rather than your father or anyone from his house when he appointed me ruler over the land… But by these slave girls you spoke of, I will be held in honor." And Michal, daughter of Saul, had no children to the day of her death." 2 Samuel 6: 20-23

Let me fill you in on some things that happened in this story before we came to this point with David and Michal. Michal was David's first wife. 1 Samuel 18:20-21 tells us that Michal was in love with David and Saul wanted his daughter to be a snare to David. Saul became more and more afraid of David to the point that David had to flee without Michal. Saul then gave Michal to another man. In 2 Samuel 3, David was able to retrieve Michal and the story says her then husband, Paltiel, "…went with her weeping behind her all the way …" I believe it is highly possible that Michal and Paltiel were in love, otherwise he would not have followed her, weeping. Perhaps Michal had fallen out of love with David and was in love with Paltiel. We do know that she was a victim of her circumstance and of her father, Saul and her husband, David.

Let me also fill you in on David's retrieval of the Ark of the Lord. He had tried once before, unsuccessfully, to bring the Ark of the Lord back to Jerusalem. After this unsuccessful attempt, David went back to God's word and discovered God's original design for carrying the Ark. David was obviously on a tremendous spiritual high. He had what we call a 'mountaintop experience' as he went back to God's word and discovered how to bring the Ark back successfully. He could not contain himself as he celebrated that success. He wasn't just celebrating the retrieval of the Ark; he was also celebrating God's presence with him that day. I can only imagine the emotions present that day as he arrived in Jerusalem with the Ark and with God's blessing.

Michal, on the other hand, had her own expectations for how David should act or react spiritually. The scripture says she despised him. The Hebrew word is 'bazah' and is translated to disesteem which means disdain, contemptible, or think to scorn. If you remember from chapter 16, the word scorn has to do with removing yourself. The word esteem means to show honor and respect. She disesteemed David by showing no respect or honor toward his spiritual experience. She removed herself from him spiritually.

Inverse 20, David returned to his household. The Hebrew word for this is 'barak'. It is a root word and means 'to kneel' as an act of adoration toward God and as a benefit toward man. David wanted to share in and have his family benefit from the spiritual high he was experiencing. Michal rejected David's blessing, therefore rejecting God.

Michal dishonored David first of all with her expectations. Secondly, she dishonored him with her speech. She made light of his attempts to celebrate. She used the word 'distinguished' which is translated 'glorious' in the KJV. She felt he dishonored himself in the way he disrobed to wear only the linen ephod. A linen ephod was like a short skirt, apron or loin cloth and was associated with the presence of God or those who had a special relationship with God. Michal either had no understanding of David's relationship with God, or perhaps she was jealous of that relationship. Michal moved away from her ability to be a spiritual helpmeet when she dishonored David. She closed her door.

Michal should have felt privileged to be part of such a Godly event. She should have been proud to have a Godly husband who was attempting to lead his family spiritually. This was the third mistake she made. She rejected David's attempt at spiritual leadership. David held tightly, however, to his leadership role as he reminded Michal of his relationship with God and its priority in his life. He reminded her that not only would he continue to celebrate God, but even more in the future than he had that day. He also reminded Michal of his need for honor. In verse 23, David told her that he would have his honor, even if from the slave girls she spoke of. Here, we see again, how easily a man can be tempted into the arms of another woman if she is meeting needs he is not receiving at home.

We have looked carefully at the appointed role of man as spiritual leader. David reminds Michal that he was appointed by God. We see, very clearly, the wrath of God on Michal as she slapped David in the face with her dishonoring words and in turn, slapping God.

Read 2 Samuel 6:23: How did God's wrath affect Michal?

How?

The greatest privilege we have in our purpose as a helpmeet is in meeting our husband's needs spiritually. Does this mean we have to be smarter, stronger, or more spiritual so we can 'set them straight'? Absolutely not!

When our husbands begin moving toward God spiritually, the most important thing they need from us is our presence. If you sit back with your arms crossed, waiting to see if it's real, you are not present! If you try to tell him how to be spiritual, you are not present! Remember, you have to put your expectations totally aside if God is to work in his life. When you are able, with a gentle and quiet spirit to trust God's work in his life, then you are present. When you are meeting his needs mentally, emotionally, physically, and spiritually, you are present. Michal did not even try to be present in David's spiritual life. She watched from the outside with her arms crossed and formed her own conclusions. She met him with scorn as she refused to join him that day.

Secondly, we need to learn how to listen. This brings us back to that quiet spirit. As our husbands begin growing and learning, they need to be able to share their experiences without the fear of an undermining spirit from us. If your behavior is godly, and you have begun to meet his needs in the other areas, he will feel free to become the man God wants him to be. Michal jumped on David when he came in to share his joy with the household. She didn't even try to listen or understand his feelings and emotions.

Thirdly, and most importantly, we need to pray for our husbands on a daily basis. Begin by praying for yourself, as you attempt to let go of him and your expectations. This will help as you begin to give him back to God.

Not every woman has a husband who is attempting spiritual leadership. I have listened to many women express a desire to live their lives for God, and feel that their unsaved or disobedient husbands were preventing them from the service they desired. I remind these women of the responsibility and service they have under their own roof. These women are literally on a mission field of their own. How can God use you elsewhere if you are not willing to follow His design for reaching your own husband? This may be the greatest challenge of service and ministry you will ever have and God has shown you how to do it!

> *"I urge then, first of all, that requests, prayers, intercession, and thanksgiving be made*
> *for everyone-for kings and all those in authority, that we may live quiet, peaceful lives*
> *in all Godliness and holiness. This is good and pleases God our Savior, who wants*
> *all men to be saved and come to a knowledge of the truth." 1 Timothy 2:1-4*

The key to meeting your husband's needs spiritually is honor. Michal dishonored David and experienced God's wrath in her life. She could have honored him with her presence, acceptance of his role as spiritual leader, kind communication, and prayer. The Hebrew word for honor is 'kabed'. It means to be heavy as in burdensome. Sometimes our honor may be a burden to us if we are still holding on to our expectation or feel we don't agree with their leadership. We have to be so careful not to let the heaviness lead us to act and speak as Michal did to David. 'Kabed' also is translated as numerous, rich, and honorable. These translations bring back memories of some vows I made many years ago on my wedding day. Those words were 'for better or for worse'. 'For better' is always easy. 'For worse' takes the kind of honor only the Lord can provide through us. Honor is taking away your expectations and giving that husband back to God. When you do this, you allow god to give him back to you. If you keep him from God, you will never really have him as God intended no matter how hard you try. In <u>Love is a Decision, (11)</u> Gary Smalley says, "To honor someone means to view that person as a *'priceless treasure'* and treat him or her with loving respect." He also says, "We can honor our loved ones whether they deserve it or not." Did you catch those words 'priceless treasure'? I see us as having come full circle here. The virtuous woman is considered to be a 'priceless treasure' by her husband in Proverbs 31:10. Why? She met him with respect, submission, availability, willingness, and honor as God designed. She treated *'him'* as a 'priceless treasure' and she received it in return. I hope and pray that you are ready to honor your husband as you accept the work God has begun in him, for better or for worse. If you are meeting his needs mentally with respect, emotionally with submission, and physically with willingness and availability, then you are icing the cake with your honor as you support and encourage him spiritually.

Several years ago, a good friend gave me a prayer for your husband. Its origin is anonymous, but the author is God himself as the prayer is completely scripture. Therefore, you are praying God's expectations for your husband and not your own. This will help to lead you away from any selfish expectations you might be tempted to pray. You need to be a daily intercessor for your husband. I hope you will begin to pray at least a portion of this prayer each day. God always hears your prayers and when you pray His word, you know you are praying His will for your life. Isn't that fantastic?

A Prayer for my Husband
Anonymous

Dear Father,

I pray for my husband today...

Monday:

That you would surround him with favor as a shield. (Psalm 5:12) May you open his ears to hear your voice; may you open his eyes to see your guidance; and may you open his heart to receive your wisdom. May you give him a spirit of wisdom and of revelation in the knowledge of you, and may the eyes of his heart be enlightened, so that he may know what is the hope of your calling, what are the riches of the glory of your inheritance in the saints, and what is the surpassing greatness of your power toward us who believe. (Ephesians 1:17-19) I bind the spirits of rebellion, stubbornness, and doublemindedness far from him in the name of Jesus, that he may be free to walk in your ways, and that he may be stable in all his ways. (James 1:8)

Tuesday:

That you will give him fresh insight and inspiration to do his work; and that you will renew his strength as the eagle's.(Isa. 40:31) May you surround him with angelic protection in every place he goes, (Psalm 91:11) and may you bring victory to him in every place the sole of his foot treads. (Josh. 1:3) May you prosper him in every task that he puts his hand to, and may he be fruitful in all he undertakes, as he seeks the counsel of wise men and delights and meditates in your word. (Psalm 1:1-3) As he delights inYou, may you give him the desires of his heart. (Psalm 37:4)

Wednesday:

I bind the spirits of pride, spiritual blindness, self-sufficiency and self-righteousness far from him in the name of Jesus, in order that he may be quick to give you all the glory for what You are doing in his life. I bind the spirits of philosophy, deception, and religious tradition far from him in the name of Jesus, so that he will not be deluded or pulled off the path that You have chosen for him. (Col. 2:8) and so that he may attain to all the wealth that comes from the full assurance of understanding, resulting in a true knowledge of God's mystery, that is Christ Himself, in whom are hidden all the treasures of wisdom and knowledge. (Col. 2:2-3) May wisdom enter his heart, and may knowledge be pleasant to his soul; may discretion guard him, and understanding watch over him, to deliver him from the way of evil. (Prov. 2:10-12) May he trust in you with all his heart, and not lean on his own understanding; may he acknowledge You in all his ways, and may you make his paths straight. (Proverbs 3:5-6)

Thursday:

In the name of Jesus, I also bind the spirits of procrastination, laziness, complacency, and foolishness far from him, so that he will not be delayed or diverted from moving ahead with You in the works that You have already created for him to accomplish. (Eph. 2:10) May he not be carnally minded, which is death, but may he be spiritually minded, which is life and peace. (Romans 8:6) May he be filled with the knowledge of your will in all spiritual wisdom and understanding, so that he may walk in a manner worthy of You, to please You in all respects, bearing fruit in every good work and increasing in the knowledge of You; strengthened with all power according to Your glorious might, for the attaining of all steadfastness and patience; joyously giving thanks to You, who have qualified us to share in the inheritance of the saints in light. (Col. 1:9-12)

Friday:

May you give him a deep thirst for Your word, and may You give him a strong hunger to move in the power of the Holy Spirit. Father, I know that you will lead him into all truth by your spirit, (John 16:13) so I can thank You and praise You and have confidence that since You have begun a good work in him, You will complete it. ((Phil 1:6) You will cause him to excel in all that he puts his hand to, as I trust You to guide him, since it is not by might, nor by power, but by your spirit. (Zech. 4:6) Help him to sharpen his awareness of spiritual things, so that he will be effective in his role as the spiritual head of our household. (Ephesians 5:23) Help me to submit to his leadership in a way that is pleasing to you. (Col. 3:18) May our love abound still more and more in real knowledge and all discernment, and may we be filled with the fruit of righteousness which comes through Jesus Christ, to the glory and praise of God. (Phil 1:9-11)

Saturday:

May the words of his mouth and the meditations of his heart be acceptable in Your sight, O Lord. (Psalm 19:14) May he be slow to anger, and not be quick-tempered, (Proverbs 14:29) and may he have a soothing tongue. (Proverbs 15:4) May you give him his heart's desire, and not withhold the request of his lips. (Psalm 21:2) May you make him to know your ways, O Lord, may you teach him Your paths, and may You make him to know your covenant. (Psalm 25:14) May you hide him in the secret place of your presence from the conspiracies of man, and may you keep him secretly in a shelter from the strife of tongues. (Psalm 31:20) When he is tempted, I thank You that You will always provide the way of escape, that he may be able to endure it. (1 Cor. 10:13)

In the name of Jesus,

Amen

Sunday:

Thank God for your husband by praying the entire prayer. Better, yet, pray the entire prayer everyday

Study Questions

Part One

Chapter 1:

What are the three virtues for the foundation of a virtuous woman?

How did Ruth display these qualities?

Chapter 2:

Our husbands can _____ in us and have no need of _____ when we accept God's _____ for our _____.

Chapter 3:

We do our husbands _____ and not _____ by accepting our place in God's _____ of _____.

Chapter 4:

She worketh willingly with her (_____) hands.

What is submission?

The Hebrew translation for hands in this verse refers to a _____ hand.

What is necessary for perfect submission?

Wrapping It Up: Meeting His Needs Mentally

When a wife is able to accept God's purpose for her creation and her position in God's chain of command, she is meeting her husband's needs mentally by showing _____.

If we are to respect our husbands, we must be careful not to give way to _____.
(1 Peter 3:4-6)

What fears could prevent you from showing respect toward your husband?

Study Questions

Part Two

Chapter 6:

1. The woman in Proverbs 31:15 rose early to take care of her family because she knew the needs of her family. How well do you believe you know the needs of your husband and family?

2. Where are you unwilling to sacrifice for what you know about the needs of your husband? Why?

3. What do you remember about the words you said to your husband when you took the vows of marriage?

Where are you failing in those vows and why?

4. Go back and read Ruth 3:2-8: Where was Boaz when Ruth went and lay at his feet to express her desire for marriage and his part as her kinsman-redeemer?

Why was he spending the night at the threshing floor?

Boaz and Ruth were both willing to make sacrifices to protect and win what was rightfully theirs.

**Nothing worth having is available without some measure of sacrifice:

____ I agree/why?

____ I disagree/why?

Chapter 7

1. What is a 'heart attitude' of submission?

2. Why is a 'heart attitude' of submission the most difficult?

3. What do you believe you have learned so far that changes your opinion of the word, 'submission'? Why?

4. Have you had a time in the past week when you were excited or perhaps had a 'good' feeling about trying to be submissive in an area of your marriage where you have possibly been selfish in the past?

Scale of 1 to 10?

What do you feel you need to do to change this number? Be specific!!!!

Chapter 8:

1. Why is it important for us to 'gird' up the loins of our minds as wives and mothers?

2. How can we do this?

3. Where do you believe you are being effective in this area?

4. Where do you feel you may need to work harder at this attempt to free your mind of unnecessary thoughts?

Chapter 9:

1. What benefits have you begun to see at this point in your study?

2. Which part of God's design for marriage do you struggle with the most? Why?

* Is anyone willing to share the prayer they wrote?

Chapter 10:

1. What does the 'closed' hand represent?

    How can you apply that to your lifestyle today?

2. What does the 'open' hand represent?

    How can you apply that to your lifestyle today?

Wrapping It Up: Meeting His Needs Emotionally

1. What is necessary if we are to meet our husband's needs emotionally?

2. Where do you believe you are in your 'quest' towards submission on a scale of 1 to 10?

What do you feel you need to do to change this number? Be specific!!!!

Study Questions

Part Three

Chapter 11:

1. How do you currently use your 'open' and 'closed' hands to reach out to others?

2. How could you improve on using your 'open' and 'closed' hands to reach out to others?

Chapter 12:

1. Where and how are you encouraging your children and husband spiritually?

2. Where and how can you improve on the spiritual encouragement you are providing?

Chapter 13:

1. How are you currently making your home a temple for God and your family?

2. Where do you think you might be pushing God and your family aside in your home?

Chapter 14:

1. What did you learn about the gates in chapter 4 of Ruth?

2. The Hebrew word for 'gate' in Ruth chapter 4, is Sha'ar (shah' ar) and it means *'door' or opening!!!* Wow! Another word that keeps popping up!! Leah's decision to 'open' the door between God and Benjamin helped him to become known at the 'door' of the city!! The same happened with Ruth and Boaz. Leah and Benjamin are fictional characters but Ruth and Boaz were real people who lived to discover the connection between a godly woman and her husband.

How do you see the connection between you and your husband in relation to the 'doors' in your marriage?

3. Read 1 Peter 3:1-2: Write, again, what it is you need to do in order to 'open' the door for your husband?

4. Read Philippians 1:6:

Who began the work in your husband?

Who will finish that work in him?

Chapter 15:

1. What was Joseph's response to Mary's God-given calling in Matthew 1: 19?

2. Who changed Joseph's heart?

3. Read Philippians 1:6: Who is going to complete the work begun in you through your callings?

4. Where do you believe you are getting in God's way right now in your life because of lack of trust in God's timing?

Study Questions

Part Four

Chapter 16:

Based on what you learned from this chapter and scripture, how would you offer 'godly' advice to someone experiencing abuse in her marriage?

Chapter 17:

1. Write Ephesians 4:29:

What should NEVER come out of our mouths?

What should ALWAYS come out of our mouths?

2. What does the word 'cleave' mean in Matthew 19:5?

Who is commanded to 'cleave'?

Who gave the 'command'?

Who is responsible for 'allowing' him to 'cleave'?

Where are you succeeding?

Where are you failing?

Chapter 18:

1. Has there been a time when you missed a 'beep' from God concerning a family member? Why?

2. Has there been a time when you received a 'beep' from God because you were observing the steps of your family?

3. What, exactly, does it mean to stay in 'beeper' range and why is it important?

Chapter 19:

1. Name some things that keep you from following this design for becoming 'uniquely woman' and tell why:

Example-pride, because my human nature causes me to feel I should have something more to offer.

2. Do you truly feel that you have it all, or does all of 'it' have you?

What are the 'its' in your life that are holding you back from following this design for becoming 'uniquely' woman?

Chapter 20:

Free discussion time to share how God has begun to change you and your marriage through this study of God's word and God's design for marriage.

What is the legacy you believe you would leave if God took you home today?

Wrapping It Up: Meeting His Needs Spiritually

1. Review:

We meet our husband's needs mentally through _____.

We meet our husband's needs emotionally through _____.

We meet our husband's needs physically through _____ and _____.

2. We meet our husband's needs spiritually through _____.

How did Michal dishonor David?

How do you believe you have shown 'honor' to your husband recently?

How do you believe you may have dishonored him recently

Bibliography

(1) Chapter 1-Holman Bible dictionary

(2) Chapter 2-<u>The Desires of a Woman's Heart</u> by Beverly LaHaye

(3) Chapter 3-Elisabeth Elliot

(4) Chapter 4-<u>The Desires of a Woman's Heart</u> by Beverly LaHaye

(5) Chapter 5-Adrian Rogers, Love Worth Finding Ministries

(6) Chapter 11-<u>My Utmost for His Highest</u> by Oswald Chambers

(7) Meeting His Needs Physically-James Dobson, "Focus on the Family" Radio

(8) Meeting His Needs Physically-<u>My Utmost for His Highest</u> by Oswald Chambers

(9) Chapter 19-<u>The Desires of a Woman's Heart</u> by Beverly LaHaye

(10) Chapter 20-Elisabeth Elliot

(11) Meeting His Needs spiritually-<u>Love is a Decision</u> by Gary Smalley

$\mathcal{M}$emory $\mathcal{V}$erses

Write out each verse below. Cut them apart for references as you memorize throughout the study.

1. Matthew 10:39	2. 1 Corinthians 11:8-9
3. 1 Corinthians 11:3	4. Ephesians 5:24
5. Jeremiah 33:3	6. Matthew 7:12

7. 1 Peter 1:13

8. Matthew 5:15

9. Philippians 4:19

10. Matthew 5:16

11. Deuteronomy 11:18-20

12. Titus 2:4-6

13. 1 Peter 3:1-2

14. 1 Thessalonians 5:24

15. 2 Corinthians 12:10

16. Ephesians 4:29

17. Romans 3:23

18. Matthew 5:5

About the Author:

My name is Cathy McBride. I am currently a second grade teacher at Pleasant Hill Elementary School in Olive Branch, Mississippi. I have been teaching for over twenty years. I have been married to Mark for twenty eight years. Mark is a retired football coach and currently teaches Driver's Education at Olive Branch High School. We have one daughter, Anna-Catherine. She is a sophomore at Belmont University in Nashville where she is a Commercial Music major. We have a dachshund, Lucy, who loves chasing golf balls and rules the house. We enjoy quality time together as a family, camping, traveling, and playing. We all love to read and enjoy sharing books and bible studies with each other. We are also members of First Baptist Church, Olive Branch.

In the beginning of my life as a wife, I began praying that God would show me His truth about marriage and His design according to scripture. Not only did He answer my prayer, but He also poured His teachings into me through this study as a way of reaching other women. I have used this study over the past thirteen years to mentor women and have marveled over what God is able to do in our lives when we are willing to take this 'walk unto death' as women of God. I believe God is now ready for *you* to find His truth in the pages of this unique study. You will meet our fictional character, Leah, as she takes you through her life and as she learns the principles and precepts we find in God's design for our lives as women. She will help you understand this design as you see it lived out in her life.

I am praying for you as you begin to take your 'walk unto death' and discover the life God intends for you when you are willing to lose yourself for His sake.

Cathy McBride
Matthew 10:39